MY LIFE, MY FOOTBALL

ANDRIY
SHEVCHENKO

with Alessandro Alciato

TRANSLATED FROM THE ITALIAN BY MARK PALMER

First published in Great Britain in 2023
This edition published 2023 by
BACKPAGE

www.backpagepress.co.uk
@BackPagePress

Italian edition first published 2021
© 2021 Baldini + Castoldi s.r.i. – Milano

ISBN: 9781909430587
eBook ISBN: 9781909430594

Typeset by BackPage
Cover design by Kouki Gharra (kulbirgharra.com)

Front cover image: Getty Images for Laureus
Printed in Great Britain by MBM Print

Andriy

To my father. I miss you so much. I wish you could see how your grandchildren are growing up.

To my children. Always try things, so that you do not have regrets. Never be afraid of failing. I will always love you; I will support you, walking by your side. Show kindness, respect and integrity.

Alessandro

To Niccolo and Allegra, the light of my life.
To all those who throw away the handbook.
Who says you can't live on emotion and instinct?

CONTENTS

FOREWORD

In this book, Sheva tells all about himself. He also tells all about us. Together, we rode a rollercoaster of emotions, sharing every extreme this game can offer.

We experienced that magical night in Manchester in 2003. Milan v Juventus for the Champions League trophy: me against my past, him in full control of his own present. Every now and then, I still picture him there, looking at the referee and then the ball, back to the referee, then the ball again. Then referee, ball, Gigi Buffon... right before he struck the decisive penalty. The kick that brought us the Champions League: 11 metres of pure joy.

Old Trafford was already known as the Theatre of Dreams – we just borrowed it for a night, but it will remain forever in our hearts. Printed in the annals of footballing history. We pass the memories down. Sheva wrote the very last word of that success story. Me and him, meanwhile, never reached a full stop: we became friends. We shared the torment of Istanbul in 2005, that city of two continents, the border town between two worlds. The rise and fall against Liverpool. The good and the bad. The rule of the strong, and the incomprehensibility of fate. We won, then we drew, and in the end we lost. Regulation time, extra time, penalties. But more than that, the aftermath. That's when we were really a team. That's when Sheva and those like him rose again, after all the tears and questions had run out. The footballing gods were playing The Beatles that night in Turkey, but we would strum again ourselves.

We loved one another and still do, very much, but we have also had cross words, perhaps because of a virtue that we share: we always say what we think. How many times did he come knocking on my door at Milanello?

"Carlo, you put me on the bench and you were wrong."

"No, I was right."

"You were wrong."

"I was right."

"You were wrong."

"I was right."

On each occasion, we could have carried on like that until the end of time. I'd put on my most serious expression. Then he would leave my office and I'd burst out laughing, like when you've just had an argument with your kids.

At a certain point in his career, Sheva was really suffering with the pain in his back. I immediately understood the source of the problem, and I didn't need a second opinion.

After every big Milan win, the team would carry me on their shoulders, throwing me into the air then catching me on the way back down. And I wasn't exactly a twig.

Carlo Ancelotti

I WAS BORN IN THE SOVIET UNION – I WILL DIE IN UKRAINE

I WAS sleeping. At 3.30am, people are asleep. The lucky ones have sweet dreams, continuing to live even with their eyes shut. Sleep can be nicer than reality, at least until your phone starts ringing. A punch in the chest that throws you out of bed.

My phone lit up at 3.30am on February 24, 2022. On the other end of the line was a familiar voice that seemed somehow different to normal. It was my mum. She was sobbing.

"Andriy…"

"Mum, what's going on?"

"It's started, Andriy."

"What's started?"

"Russia, Russia."

I didn't understand, or rather I didn't want to. And yet, in the preceding days, we had all seen unequivocal signs. Clues about a new, terrible, opaque horizon.

"Mum, stay calm."

"Andriy, the Russians have invaded. We are at war."

She was speaking from Kyiv and I was listening in London. She was at home, and I was in my home away from home. The noise of mortar bombs and silence: a sudden imbalance between sounds and feelings.

I felt like I was dying, being sucked into a devastating, explosive black hole inside myself. Anger, sadness, fear, courage, a sense of impotence: everything mixed together in an internal earthquake.

"Mum, please don't cry."

She couldn't give me what I wanted. The world that she had known up until that point was changing shape. All around her, the map of Ukraine was crumpling. Her country. My country. Our country.

"Andriy, I felt our building shake because of the explosions."

"I'm coming straight there. I'm going to chuck a few things in a case and leave."

"No, my son, go on television and tell them what's happening. The world needs to know."

We said goodbye and it was the worst moment of my life. Nothing will ever be worse or even remotely comparable. It was the start of a terrible, lightning-quick agony.

I felt guilty. A few days before, it had been my mum's birthday and I had booked flights to Kyiv, going out on February 19 and returning 10 days later. Because I had a few bureaucratic matters to take care of in England, I had delayed my departure until the 26th. Forty-eight hours after that accursed phone call. An unforgivable delay.

I should have been in Kyiv, not to celebrate with her but to defend her. A son needs to act as a shield for his mother, even when the bullets are real.

I turned on the television and put on BBC News. I could now see what my mum had been describing. Pieces of the puzzle, evidence of death. In that precise moment, I stopped sleeping. I couldn't allow myself to waste a second, to not know how my friends and family, my city, were doing. If they responded when I phoned, it meant they were alive. The time between one call and the next seemed infinite, a lacerating pain in the soul.

"Bye mum, we'll speak later."

I was well aware that 'later' might not exist. That it might be destroyed by an attack that the anti-air raid signals had not managed to pick up. Every 'speak later' could actually be a 'goodbye', the last salute before the lights went off.

For me, it was a devastating period. People sent me hundreds of videos. I watched them all and felt my skin splitting, as if the debris flying around on film had actually struck me. I saw missiles knocking down our buildings, bridges collapsing, Russian helicopters polluting the sky and people's lives, and then people, so many people, who were losing everything and trying to escape. Thousands of them, all running for their lives.

How can I help?
How can I put an end to all this?
I'm rich and famous; could my money contribute to peace?
Putin has blood on his hands. How can people not realise this?
Is there a way to make myself useful?
I want to stop the war, but how?

For three months, these painful refrains ran through my mind. I was no longer lucid. Far away from my family and friends but also from the man I used to be. Tears were my constant companion and every now and then I would vent at my wife.

"I just don't know what to do."

In the meantime, I continued to beg my mum to come to London.

"No, Andriy, this is my home."

The same response came from my sister.

The invaders had reckoned on it being a short, sharp war. The rapid theft of a country. They wanted to steal Ukraine and her history, but they didn't succeed because they hadn't taken into account the sense of belonging in our people.

As time went by, I hit upon a few responses of my own, but the path – especially the internal one – was long and tortuous. I was engaged by the Ukrainian president, Volodymyr Zelensky, a hero among heroes, a man who from the very first second of the war undertook not to abandon his people and his country. Just like my mum and sister.

Zelensky made me the first ambassador of United 24, the state-run fundraising charity. I wasn't a soldier, but I began fighting with the weapons that I had: words. Lots of people love me; they listened to what I said and then they helped. I also went back to Ukraine – the first time via an almost 20-hour train journey from Poland. I spent most of it lost in silent thought. And strong, strong emotions.

When the soldiers checking passenger documentation recognised me, I could see the pride in their eyes. It was the happiness of being that little bit less alone. I was counting down to when I would be back in my city's warm embrace.

Over time, I have begun returning to Kyiv more frequently. You don't need to be scared of going through your own front door, even when it has become a target.

In a bar, I saw a soldier stroking his little daughter's

hands and saying: "My love, I need to go but I will be back soon." Deep down, the soldier knew that could turn out to be a lie, but it needed to be said. Who knows just how hard it was for him to utter those words; how much internal pain it caused.

In Dnipro, I visited the paediatric department of a hospital and saw six- or seven-year-old kids with terrible wounds. I listened to the stories of the bombs that had hit their homes and taken away their legs, their arms, their families. I went from room to room, from story to story, from suffering to suffering, until I couldn't go on. I'm the father of four sons. But then I realised it would not be right to simply turn and walk away. I carried on, but it was hard.

I also went to Irpin, where the Russians had opened fire on fleeing civilians. There were so many deaths that the bodies were left on the street; there simply wasn't the capacity to take them all away. I noticed two boys playing football in a destroyed stadium. They were dribbling the ball between the enormous craters caused by the bombs. In front of the collapsed stands. A few metres from the destroyed dressing rooms.

Every now and then, they would stop to pick up these strange rocks from the ground. They were pieces of the exploded bombs. But despite everything, they were having fun.

I gave them two new footballs.

"Thank you, Sheva."

"No, thank you. Today you taught me a lot."

Watching them, I had understood that the stadium was a symbol. It needed to be preserved and reconstructed, as did many others like it. I managed to raise all the necessary funds for this reconstruction phase. As a kid, I had played many games and scored dozens of goals on that pitch for the Dynamo Kyiv youth teams. I wasn't yet an established champion. I hadn't yet won the Ballon d'Or. I hadn't yet lifted the Champions League trophy. I was just a kid from the Kyiv suburbs.

I was born in the Soviet Union but I will die in Ukraine. Me and my country are one and the same. In this book, I'll explain why.

CHERNOBYL, REACTOR NO.4

It was radioactive. My football was radioactive. It was burning, dissolving, crumpling in on itself. It stank – that stench you get when cheap plastic is thrown on the flames. The air was going out of it. It was suffocating, dying. I had brought a little piece of Chernobyl into the family home. A small atomic bomb, hidden away inside my greatest passion.

At the age of nine, I had just unwittingly introduced an invisible threat to the small apartment I shared with my parents and older sister Elena.

My father, Nikolay, didn't seem too worried. Or rather, he *was* worried, we just didn't realise. He was in the army, where they taught you to hide your emotions. He observed that impromptu fire in silence, tightly gripping a strange device in his hands. I'd never seen it before, but it was used to measure radiation levels, in the air and in objects themselves. My mother, Lubov, wasn't speaking either. She was instantly protective, in a way that only women know how to be when they perceive their children to be at risk.

With my father's help, she had set fire to the football, after throwing it into a basin. Perhaps this wasn't the best way to get rid of other people's sins, but hers was certainly the most immediate idea to try to dissolve the devil's tracks.

On April 26, 1986, reactor No.4 at the Chernobyl nuclear plant exploded, and it was like the whole world had been blown up. However, the true, devastating reach of the incident would only become clear over time. To begin with, I didn't realise anything was wrong, not least because only a few days later, most of the people in Kyiv were out on the streets to celebrate May 1, Labour Day.

The seriousness of the situation was totally unknown to me initially. I went about my business as if no danger existed. I continued to have fun in my restricted – dare I say intimate – little boundary, less than 150 kilometres from that living hell.

In theory, 150km is a long way, but not when we're talking about thin air. What you're left with is an unhindered motorway on which the bad stuff can travel. A tunnel full of wind and poisons, which ended up everywhere: on the living-room sofa where my mother and father slept; in the little bedroom I shared with my sister, in the small, dignified kitchen of our apartment.

In front of our block, there was a building where the boilers were housed. At the rear, they had put a football goal, and me and my friends spent hours and hours playing there. We never tired, and we similarly never got bored of going to reclaim the balls that ended up on the roof because of a wonky shot. As the most agile member of our group, that task often fell to me. To get up there, you had to climb a tree then jump onto the roof. It was a risky manoeuvre, but it always went well for me.

Right up until that day. And to think that I'd been so happy, because I had found a number of other balls in addition to my own. A good number, in fact. The remnants of forgotten games, inherited from kids who hadn't had the courage to attempt the climb up the tree. Had I not seen one of my own on fire shortly afterwards, I'd have called it the ball cemetery.

My ball was buried in a basin. When I walked through the front door, it had been tucked under my arm like a treasured trophy. I'd had to fight to get it back. I saw my dad there waiting for me.

"Andriy, give me the ball."

"Why?"

"Just give it to me."

I asked no further questions, and my father didn't say much either. He had spent 12 years in Germany, and then from the autumn of 1975 to the spring of 1976 he had been posted to Ayagoz, in what is now Kazakhstan, in a base that hosted several military garrisons and a group of rocket troops. After that, he was recalled to Kyiv.

He was an expert in the art of silence, both on account of his own character and the orders of his superiors. And when it came to the matter in hand, he knew what he was doing. He was probably one of the few to have guessed that something was up, even as the authorities told their lies, sought to hide things and looked for solutions that were always going to be impossible to find.

I did what had been asked. At that point, my father applied the radiation meter which immediately showed some terrifying levels. The indicators went mad – either the thing was broken, or we were all about to be broken ourselves, crushed and dismantled by clouds that may have been colourless but were certainly not painless.

They were full of particles so small that they could attack you from the inside. In the meantime, they had given my ball a kicking and so my family had decided to condemn it to the flames.

However, let me repeat: at this point, I knew nothing, even if a few things around us were changing as the days went on. I noticed that they no longer let us walk along the streets and that they were always washing the pavements and even the front of the buildings.

Only at the end of March – a month after the catastrophe – did Moscow announce what was to be done. 'Evacuate the children.' Parents were given a little bit of notice by the authorities; told where their children would be taken. An address. There was no panic, just this new reality constructed by the will of those in charge.

The schools were shut. Coaches arrived in Kyiv from all over the Soviet Union and kids aged between six and 15 were taken away. The bus I got on took me to the train station, where I began a 10-hour journey to Mar d'Azov, a northern part of the Black Sea coast, 1500 kilometres from home. It felt like an adventure or a school trip.

Our final destination was a kind of summer camp, divided up into dorms. There were seven of us in each one, so far away from our homes, still unaware of the true reality of Chernobyl, just hoping to be lucky. Radiation does not follow a fixed path, from point A to point B. You don't know where and when it's going to rain, and so where the particles will land. You don't know which way the wind is blowing. You just have to cross your fingers.

I remember the enormity of the place, the vast

dimensions. Perhaps the choice of location wasn't entirely random – when there is no visible horizon, it's more difficult to focus your anxiety (however sub-conscious) on a fixed point. It just drifts away, towards who knows where.

I can't say it was a bad time, just a strange one. We did some studying, but above all I played football. Every single day, with the teammates who had been taken away from their families alongside me. I also played other sports: tennis, athletics, basketball.

After a month, and after collecting my sister who had been evacuated to a different camp with her school, my parents arrived on the Black Sea. We had another three weeks there together before heading back to my grandparents' house in Dvirkivshchyna in the Yagotinsky district of the Kyiv region, where we spent the rest of the summer. All things considered, I had fun in that period, just as I had in Kyiv before the Chernobyl tragedy forced us into exile.

In March, just before we were evacuated, Dynamo Kyiv had chosen me to join their youth section on the back of how I performed in a school tournament.

I attended School 216 (Soviet schools all had numbers, not names) – a grey, three-storey building in Obolon, a district on the outskirts of Kyiv that had only been in existence for a few years but had all the necessary things: a nursery, a school, a sports centre, a cinema, a park, a doctor's surgery.

Oleksandr Shpakov, Dynamo's youth team coach, had come to watch the tournament. He was also the person who then organised our Black Sea transfer in our hour of need.

I didn't have a defined role on the pitch. I ran forwards and back, basically playing everywhere. I defended, then I moved into the middle, then I set my sights on the opposition net and scored goals.

Before then, I had never played a proper 11 v 11 match. I'd never played a game with a referee, two goalkeepers or on grass. Our pitch was basically a clay court. I was used to contests without rules, where it was a matter of pure heart, and where the winners were the team who weren't overcome by tiredness or called in for dinner by their mums.

It was rarely a hard job to find me: you just had to look around the grounds close to where we lived. I fantasised about being either Oleh Blokhin or Oleksandr Zavarov, both of them attackers.

I don't remember exactly when my love of football began. What I do know is that meeting Shpakov changed my life. At the end of one of the games in that tournament, he came over, introduced himself and handed me a slip of paper. "This has my name, address and telephone number. Get your parents to call me. Would you like to go for a trial at Dynamo?"

This was a rhetorical question, but the response was up to my folks. I immediately went back home. Dad didn't seem very interested, while mum replied with a question.

"Do you want to go?"

"Yes, it's Dynamo Kyiv…"

"Well go then."

Dad complied. "Ok, go and try."

Mum contacted the coach, who gave us all the details. It was her who took me along to the trial. She knew I didn't want anything else. She loved me.

To uncover the next generation of talent, Shpakov did the rounds of the schools but he also watched kids just playing football in the street. He left no stone unturned.

He had us play a game and do a few skills drills. Deep inside, I felt I was better than any of the other kids and after a few minutes, that impression had given way to certainty. Two of us ended up being picked. In the end, it wasn't all that exciting.

The really emotional thing was crossing the threshold of the Dynamo Kyiv academy for the first time. Outside, the club logo loomed large. Inside, the pitches were perfect, while the dressing rooms were the best I had ever seen (not just because I had never seen any before that point).

There was netting in place to stop people spying from the outside – we felt protected. We watched the older lads, the ones who sooner or later would make their debuts in the first team, turn professional, play in the league and maybe even the European competitions.

It didn't last long. Only a few training sessions. Then reactor No.4 exploded.

AND WHAT OF DYNAMO?

THE SEPTEMBER after the Chernobyl disaster, the schools opened up again and I was focused on other things, even if every now and then I asked myself: *And what of Dynamo?* I never answered the question, leaving the doubt there, hanging. I was absent-minded, careless, untidy, forgetful. My head was an utter mess, a tangle of juvenile thoughts.

And what of Dynamo? As soon as the thought occurred, it would slip from my mind.

And what of Dynamo? A single second later, I would change the subject.

And what of Dynamo? Hmm.

Even though football was the north star for my whole journey, I couldn't remember what I had been thinking even a moment earlier.

Football came looking for me. Football wanted me. Football opened my eyes when the light threatened to go out or I was tempted to look elsewhere. Football made allies with my destiny. It called me back. Or rather, it called my mother back, as I found out one afternoon.

"Andriy, your coach called."

"What coach, mum?"

"The one from the trial, remember?"

"Ah yes, what did he say?"

"He wants you to rejoin the team."

"Can I?"

"You can, Andriy, you can."

Had Shpakov not recontacted my mum, my football career would already have been over and I would have disappeared inside a toxic cloud, even before all the drama at Chernobyl. Of the kids that I grew up with, only one is still alive. Two, if I count myself.

I was saved by sport and my parents, or at least they showed me the way. I did well to grasp the opportunity and not succumb to temptation.

The Soviet Union, with its 15 socialist republics, was still in existence at that point. But already you could see the cracks that would lead to it falling apart five years later. There were black holes that expanded to swallow all those kids with whom I had such fun growing up.

Drugs, alcohol, guns: that's what killed them. They were always fighting a losing battle: at a certain point, people stopped believing in anything and just gave up. In criminality – of the most violent kind – they saw the only way to get by.

The police couldn't help anyone because often they were corrupt. Enemy upon enemy in a merciless kingdom. There was no such thing as light: just different degrees of black. Everyone I knew began going down the wrong path around the age of 12. They paid the price for the sins of a country that was falling apart at the seams. I grew up with them. They invited me into their homes. I knew all their names and faces. I spent many hours playing football, but my spare time was spent with those boys. It was my good fortune not to go down the wrong path.

But in the jungle you can be attacked when you least expect it, and you're left with two options: you either give in or you defend yourself against the beasts. It happened to me twice.

The first time, I came home with a broken nose, a split lip and in excruciating pain. I'd ended up in the middle of a fight and my mother struggled to recognise me. For a whole week, I wasn't allowed out, and from that moment on I have hated violence. I've been around it enough to know it when I see it.

I've done what I can to help people. Like during the 2006 World Cup in Germany. A few days before the tournament began, one of my childhood friends came out of prison after a seven-year sentence. I helped find him a job, then arranged through the Ukrainian federation to get him along to our matches as a guest, so he could sample the atmosphere of the most incredible tournament in football.

As far as we could, we made him feel like one of us. Many years ago, I had said to him: "If you carry on living this kind of life, I'll be forced to put some distance between us."

"Andriy, this is just the way I am."

"People can always change."

"It's too late for me."

He wasn't even 18 years old at that stage. And so, that's exactly what I did, without ever stopping loving him or keeping abreast of his situation.

In Germany, he seemed different. He was happy to

be there with me, not just as a welcome guest but as my great friend. His happiness was my happiness, because his suffering had been my suffering.

Every time one of them fell, a wound opened up deep within me, because I knew one of us had gone. He died, too, in an accident not long after the World Cup. They tried to operate on him, but discovered that his liver had been compromised by years of substance abuse. That long period in prison had further damaged his health. So, they closed him back up.

I consider myself lucky, but I also made good choices and I had the support of my parents. My father worked really hard, and my mother had a job in a nursery. They were two good people, happy for me to devote myself to sport and not be out on the streets, drinking, smoking, mugging people. Having a knife put to your throat wasn't a rare event in those days.

When Shpakov called my mother and asked me to go back to training, it set me on a defined path. The first year, because I was too young to officially sign for Dynamo, me and my teammates played for a satellite team called Tempo, in the local Kyiv league.

All our opponents were older, but we still managed to finish first. And then, finally, we got to pull on the real Dynamo jersey. We trained every day, and played in two competitions: the city league on a Saturday and the national league on a Sunday. Us kids travelled in groups of six or seven without adults. We used public transport, including the underground. From my house to the Nyvky training ground took an hour and ten minutes, to be exact. To get there and back took almost two-and-a-half hours before you factored in any hold-ups.

Sometimes in winter, to reduce the time on the way

back we'd take a shortcut through a dark wood. It was pitch black, I was really scared and jumped at the slightest noise. In the mind of a 10-year-old kid, monsters and ghosts are real. And yet even those improvised little trips taught me something useful. When you are together, you draw courage from one another.

ITALY – LOVE AT FIRST SIGHT

I BELIEVE in destiny, and mine was wrapped up in a football. When I first started playing, I forgot things, got timings wrong, left my boots at home. I was a disorganised child, particularly in my first year at Dynamo Kyiv.

Once I missed a training session because I got my days wrong. Another time, the same thing happened with a game. I turned up at the wrong place to find an empty pitch. This was a few months after I came back from the Black Sea and normal life resumed. Shpakov asked me to meet him at the training ground.

"Sit yourself down there."

He pointed towards a chair. It was just the two of us in the room.

"Listen, Andriy, this is the last time that I forgive you. The next time you make a mistake, you're off the team. I expect discipline from you. Remember this word: discipline. It will serve you well in life."

That very brief pep talk changed me forever. Just before making a mistake, I would hear my coach's words and pull hard on the brake, a centimetre from the abyss. I made a real effort to avoid missteps and it wasn't easy, because careless people aren't nasty. They just forget things that should be glued to their brains. Either that or they don't give the right importance to certain things.

Shpakov gave me a reason to concentrate. He was brilliant, a really good man. He wasn't just interested in your sporting results; in fact, these were often secondary for him. Education and growth were what counted, having respect for other people. He was a life coach even more than a football coach.

Through him, I learned to not be overbearing, to not behave in an egotistical way. I learned that things are easier as a team. Thanks to him, I learned the value of sacrifice and the beauty of humility. He didn't try to force our growth – he knew at that age, some people managed it quicker than others, both in terms of talent and physique.

He also kept an eye on our school grades, and if they weren't to his liking, he would issue penalties. You'd have to miss a session or even a whole week. This allowed our parents not to worry.

At school, I applied myself just enough to avoid Shpakov's punishments but I didn't have the patience to study at home. I ended up barely doing my homework – the only things that stayed in my head were what I heard in the classroom.

If I could go back in time, I'd apply myself a lot more. My priority was football, but there was one subject I loved: history. It carried me away. With my mind, I travelled way back in time to far-flung lands. That's where we all came from, after all. Actual travel was a challenge. Leaving the

Soviet Union was allowed only for work reasons or if you were part of a very restricted elite. Over and above these bureaucratic considerations, normal citizens just didn't have the money.

My sister was born in Potsdam in Germany and my dad was able to move around a fair bit due to his army links. From that point of view, they were more fortunate than me. I left home for the first time in March 1989 at the age of 12 to play a tournament in Italy, where I would return as a Milan footballer. I don't think that was a coincidence – I believe in fate. It exists and I have the proof.

The journey was long. With an internal passport, we travelled from Kyiv to Moscow where, after a full day's waiting, we were issued with the external ones we needed to leave the Soviet Union.

At Sheremetyevo-2 airport we boarded a flight to Rome. We landed in the morning, and that night we took a train to Naples to then board a bus that would take us the 100 kilometres to Agropoli, where the tournament was being staged.

Back in Rome, we didn't feel tired. We were as excited as anyone setting foot in a new world for the first time. We sped from one Roman sight to another with the same pace we showed on the pitch. We were crazy with joy and curiosity. Colosseum: magnificent. Piazza del Popolo: immense. St Peter's: breathtaking, and that's me speaking as an orthodox Christian.

Whichever way I looked, I saw something unique. I felt like I was right at the heart of the empire, one of the few topics on which I'd managed to fully concentrate at school. For me, Italy was love at first sight.

In the space of a few hours, my personal map had expanded its borders to Agropoli. A dream with a sea view. What struck me immediately was the kindness and generosity of the people. They were forever giving us little pats on the cheek and supporting us in our games without even knowing who we were.

We didn't have anything beyond an outsized dose of enthusiasm and a little plastic bag in which to carry our few belongings. Every minute we spent there was a discovery, even if, out on the pitch, it was our opponents who were finding out about us.

We won the tournament. In the semi-final, I scored five goals against the team from San Marino, a small and magnificent enclave within Italian borders. In the final, I bagged another five against the hosts, a side called Agropoli Railwayman's After-Work Club FC.

Our country's football federation, which for the first time had not sent a team from Moscow to compete at the tournament, had made an excellent impression. We ate pasta, mozzarella, pizza and drank Coca-Cola and Fanta – all impossible to find in the Soviet Union.

Tournament organisers and locals showered us with gifts. I got a pair of jeans which I remember to this day: blue, elegant, no patches – new. I also received a blue Diadora tracksuit and a pair of shoes. I felt like a true king.

On the sly, people also slipped us a few lire so we could buy something for our families back home. For my dad, I chose a Gillette razor; perfume for Elena and my mum. Real treasures.

As we left, I had a strong feeling that I would return to Italy. A certainty, more than anything.

You never forget your first trip, nor those that come later. Like the one to Wales in 1990 to take part in the Ian Rush Cup, named after the legendary striker who had already won two European Cups with Liverpool by that point.

I played well and scored a lot of goals, finishing as the top marksman in the competition. My prize was a pair of football boots. Ian Rush football boots. Nike, real leather, all for me. They were exactly the right size, with just one problem: in the subsequent month and a half, I had a growth spurt. The boots got too small, but I kept wearing them.

After a few weeks, holes appeared, two of them at the big toes, breaking through the end of the boots, but I didn't lose heart. At the end of each match, I shined them back up then went home to my little bedroom, took out a needle, thread and piece of leather and began to sew, covering up the signs of wear and tear.

I continued to score goals, often with a bit of my foot sticking out of my boot. The longer my feet got, the harder it became to contain them in the boots, and eventually it became an impossible task. It was only then that I reluctantly set them aside. I never threw them away, out of respect for Ian Rush, who had gifted them to me. Out of respect for Dynamo Kyiv, who had allowed me to live such an experience. Out of respect for my parents, who always worked so hard, and would never have been able to buy me those boots themselves.

Dad was a tough sort, mum a little softer. It was her job to speak to my teachers and the head of the school whenever I fell behind due to my sporting commitments. Once, when I was 13, I let her down. The day before an exam, Shpakov had told us: "If any of you finish before training is due to start, I'll be waiting down at the pitch. The others can come the following day. The exam is more important than football." I was one of the first to finish. I went home to collect my football bag then ran into some friends who invited me to go fishing with them.

"Go on, come with us, we'll have fun."

That's what I did, thinking that missing just one training session would not do any harm.

The trip lasted a few hours. When I came home, my mother was waiting for me close to our building.

"Andriy, how did training go?"

"Good, mum, good."

"Funny that, because Shpakov called, asking if you were going down to the pitch. I told him you had just left."

I was trembling. I knew I had betrayed something within myself, never mind the trust of my mum and coach (to whom I'd promised several years earlier that I would never make those same mistakes again).

"Andriy, one more thing."

"Yes, mum?"

"I'm pulling your leg. Your coach didn't call. I played a trick on you."

She had understood everything. Mums always know what's going to happen several moves in advance. They can see into their children's future.

My sense of shame was undiminished. And so I swore to myself that I would never miss a training session again. Not a single one.

THE CALL OF THE WILD

GROWING meant locating the reset button, and by now it was obvious to me that it was to be found either in the depths of the heart or the head – attached to hidden feelings or hidden truths, in those places where our dreams are formed.

I knew I wanted to become a footballer, and so I changed to pursue that objective. I was not (yet) a robot, or a computer – as people would often describe me in the years to come – but I had chosen to go down a very clear path. The way of hard work, dedication, total commitment.

Every now and then, I strayed from my path, as can happen when you feel like you're no longer a kid but you're not yet an adult. When that happened, I quickly corrected myself. I never had enough time, so I tried to fashion little extra pieces for myself. I'd get up really early in the morning so I could train before school, on my own.

Snow, rain, temperatures well below zero: if I felt I

needed to run, that's exactly what I did. My head gave the orders, my body obeyed; I tired myself out and felt good. More than pride-fuelled sprints, I saw this as a necessary marathon, and I had a favourite, quite perfect location: Lake Verbne, near Obolon, my area of Kyiv. A natural gymnasium. To improve my lung capacity, I'd keep my speed up while running 10-kilometre laps of the place. I'd use the little beaches to do muscle-strengthening exercises on the sand then I'd stop in the parks and use the weight machines to work on my adductor and abdominal muscles.

Sometimes I was tired when I arrived at school, but I was always happy. And I never fell asleep at my desk, because I was already thinking about the following morning's alarm call. If I hadn't been a footballer, I would still have become a professional sportsperson. I'm convinced that I was born an athlete. As well as training with Dynamo and organising extra practice matches with my friends, and before I dedicated myself exclusively and permanently to football, I also played basketball and tennis.

For six months, I did freestyle wrestling three times a week. In the summer, I swam in Lake Verbne, which was 20 metres deep, or sailed a catamaran. In the winter, I went sledging or even skiing on the little hills that dropped down to the water. I enjoyed downhill skiing, but preferred the cross-country version, because it was harder work. I remember all sorts of impromptu competitions, sometimes against complete strangers. I just about always won.

Had I not made the grade in the sport that made me famous, I would probably have become an ice hockey player. When the lake froze over, it became the perfect arena for matches. We used portable barriers to mark out the court and the goals, then it was a case of skates, sticks and away. We didn't use any form of protective gear and were just about always in short-sleeves: we never felt the cold.

People came down specifically to watch me and they all said the same thing: 'You should try out for a team.' In those days in Kyiv, the Sokil club – formed in 1963 – were doing well in the Soviet league.

I may have given everything for football, but for ice hockey I threw myself out of a first-floor window of the family home. It was a beautiful winter's day; one of those where the sky is clear and the colours so vivid that they tell a thousand different stories as they reflect off the snow. A collection of perfect pictures, drawn in frozen ink. I came home from school and, as usual, mum was waiting to have lunch with me.

"Andriy, how did it go today?"

"Where?" I asked, trying to buy time.

"What do you mean 'where'? In class," she insisted.

"Not great, mum," I said under my breath.

"Why?"

"We had a test and…"

"And?"

"It went badly. I'll tell you about it later, because right now I'm in a rush. After I've eaten, I'm going to the lake to play," I said, already knowing I was doomed.

"No Andriy, you're going to stay here and study, so that when your father gets home, you'll know what to tell him. Tomorrow you'll redo the test."

Every time my dad came back from his army commitments, he would ask about school. There's no way he would sit back and accept what had just happened.

After lunch, mum went back to work, a three-minute walk from our front door. And because it's good to trust and even better not to trust, she locked the door behind her, taking the keys so that there was absolutely no way I could escape.

I held out for 30 minutes in front of the books, and then the call of the wild was too strong. I just had to go to the lake. I had to. The window struck me as the perfect escape route that wouldn't leave any trace behind. I threw it open and, after checking that nobody was walking below, I launched my ice hockey stick. Luckily, I didn't kill anyone. Next up were my skates. Again, no harm done.

By now, we had reached the difficult part: throwing myself out. I didn't give it a second's thought. A quick run-up, a jump and I was down. Soaked through, having landed on the snow, but still bodily intact. At that point, I could have added skydiving without a parachute to my list of favourite sports.

I gathered up my belongings and went to meet my friends, who were waiting to begin the game. While playing and having fun, I totally lost track of time, and only realised how late it had got when the sky grew dark. I ran home as quickly as I could, all the while imagining how my parents would punish me.

I'd done badly at school, neglected my homework, escaped by throwing myself out of a window and played ice hockey without permission: I was really in for it. Above all, I feared my father's fury. The last few metres were truly terrible. I plucked up the courage to push on, and sure enough dad was waiting for me outside our building.

"Hi Andriy."

"Hi."

"Go on in."

'Here we go,' I thought. I was ready for anything. Or better, I was ready for anything except what actually happened: he forgave me. We spoke and he realised that when it came to sport, I was utterly powerless to resist. Mine was much more a mission than a whim. It was a devastating force, in the most positive way.

In the eyes of his son, he could see an almost ferocious determination, the same one he had witnessed when, for a short period, he had introduced me to artistic gymnastics, specifically high bar. It was a big passion of his and I didn't want to disappoint him. And so I twirled, flying with my body and my imagination.

I enjoyed gymnastics.

I enjoyed tennis.

I enjoyed basketball.

I enjoyed swimming.

I enjoyed sailing the catamaran.

I enjoyed downhill skiing.

I enjoyed cross-country skiing.

I enjoyed freestyle wrestling.

I enjoyed ice hockey.

A routine, a serve, a basket. A stroke, a turn, a slalom. A bit of uphill acceleration, a pin, a slap at the puck. Regardless of the discipline, I had fun and wanted to win. To achieve that, I knew I had to train non-stop, always pushing my limits.

In the end, I managed to achieve one great satisfaction in ice hockey. During a holiday to Washington around 2015, I went to the arena of the Washington Capitals to meet my friend Alexander Ovechkin, a true NHL legend. At the end of their training session, he invited me onto the ice to skate with him, and I was up to the challenge. My kids were there too. I didn't want to show myself up and he paid me real compliments.

Remember that kid at the lake whom everyone told to try out for a team? Evidently, a little bit of him remained.

Who knows whether I could have made it to the Washington Capitals as well?

I played football. And I enjoyed that too.

WE'LL GIVE YOU ONE MORE YEAR, ANDRIY

DEEP DOWN, I'm sure a few professors at Kyiv's University of Physical Education and Culture wanted me to opt for ice hockey too.

Their entry exam consisted of a test of footballing abilities. We students in search of glory and knowledge had to try our hand at some predetermined exercises – how to dribble past opponents, take a shot on goal and do keepie-uppies.

I was about to turn 16, it was summer, and those abilities suddenly failed me. This was a dull, hard blow that was rather difficult to explain away to those who asked what had happened and why.

I was still achieving excellent results with Dynamo Kyiv, but after misfiring in the exam there was going to be no university for me. And so my dad, beginning to get a little afraid on my account, laid out an alternate path.

"Andriy, you need to go and study at the military

school." He delivered this unexpected pot-shot – a painful direct hit – at a moment when I was totally disarmed, completely vulnerable. He was sitting at home with mum at his side. I was standing in front of them, trying to defend my mission, my life.

"But dad, I don't want to abandon football."

"And yet football is the very reason you didn't get into university."

He was right, but even the thought of such a resounding divorce left me feeling devastated. Taking off that Dynamo shirt would have cut me deep.

And so I repeated what I had just said, adding a little force, dialling up my courage. It wasn't always easy to go against my father.

"I don't want to abandon football. Let me decide, please."

They looked at one another and made a joint decision in that very instant.

"One year, Andriy. We'll give you one more year."

"Thank you, dad, and thank you, too, mum."

"It's right and proper that you try to follow your destiny, but if the football has not gone well in 12 months' time, you'll need to get ready for military school without any further discussion. Time is precious and needs to be utilised in the best possible way – wasting it is not allowed."

The countdown clock was already ticking down. I went on the attack once again.

Tick tock, tick tock. Each and every second could turn out to be the crucial one.

I was still playing for the youth team but they had also begun to call me up for some matches with the Dynamo reserves – just to make up the numbers or stand in for injured players. I would end up on the bench or in the stand. The most I got in those early days was a few minutes on the pitch: my first taste of the world of grown-up football.

The league was a sort of Serie B, where you not only found young guys like me, with their whole sporting life ahead of them, but opponents – and sometimes even teammates – who were rough and unpleasant. Men at the end of their careers or who had been cast aside by the biggest clubs. Men who were angry with the world and wanted to show that they had ended up here by mistake. Men playing for their last modest payday, playing to feed their families.

These were my first rehearsals as I strove for a bigger and better stage, while for them it was a swansong. It wasn't always easy to reconcile these two states of mind.

I don't know how many kicks I took. How many bruises I ended up with. These guys hit you, hard and often. Especially when it came to me, the smallest kid on the pitch. They saw it as some kind of revenge on the people who hadn't rated them: *If we didn't make it to the top, why should you get to?* They turned it into a question of pride.

But what did they know about the pact I had made with my parents? Of the 12 months that our family meeting had established would be the dividing line between all or nothing? My opponents and teammates didn't want to fail. I, on the other hand, simply *couldn't*.

It was the most real form of football that I could have experienced, and I had entered through a steel door rather than a golden gate. I began to understand what it meant to go out in search of a result; to understand just how much a victory could mean. 'Your death is my life,' as the Latin saying has it. Every second I was given on the pitch needed to be treated like an opportunity, and that's exactly what I did.

Even though they used every means available to try to stop me during the matches, I had a lot of fun. It was a great period; I even signed the first contract of my career, worth 50 dollars a month. That was one of the greatest moments of my life that brought with it great responsibility: I was now earning considerably more than my father. I set aside my first four pay-packets to buy my family a TV and VHS video recorder – luxury items like that had never entered our home. However, I was well aware that I had still achieved nothing at this point.

The man responsible for ensuring that we kept our good sense and concentration was Volodymyr Onyshchenko, the reserve team coach. He had been a brilliant striker, scoring twice in the 1975 Cup Winners' Cup final when Dynamo defeated Ferencvaros. He had also played against Pele and won 44 caps for the Soviet Union.

Having just turned 16, I moved permanently to his care, saying goodbye to the youth section and, in a certain sense, the care-free nature of those years. I no longer had Shpakov, who had accompanied me on my first trip to Italy, nor Oleksandr Lysenko, the man who had replaced him. It was he who had taken me on my final trip as a youth team player. That one was to Italy as well. The destination of my destiny, you could say.

In the same summer of 1992 that they blocked my admission to the university, we went to play a tournament near Milan. We won that one too, and I was named the tournament's best player.

Above all, I had the chance to visit San Siro, a place I had only seen on television and even then in the grainy images that made their way to Kyiv in those days. Yet even though the quality of the transmission was so poor, that stadium had always fascinated me. It struck me as magical, mysterious. In a certain sense, it was almost better to have only seen a little of it. When the right moment came, there would be many more corners to discover, a wider array of emotions to experience.

That opportunity arose during one of our rest days at the tournament. We asked Lysenko to take us into the city – to San Siro, specifically. He used his contacts to get us into the stadium and as soon as I set foot in that place, something went off inside me. My mind was spinning as I struggled to control my thoughts, one in particular: *One day I'm going to play here.*

I was almost moved to tears – an intimate moment that even I struggled to understand. I was hypnotised by the majesty of the place. The pitch was perfect and immense, and the stands had a noble, elegant appearance. I looked at the four towers at the corners, mapping out the stadium perimeter, and imagined the same number of silos in which you could store the balls used to score the most beautiful goals. A museum inside a museum. History inside history.

I couldn't predict the future, but I could feel its vibrations, just like when the fans get on their feet and chant in chorus: "If you don't jump up and down, you're a *Nerazzurro* clown." Standing there inside San Siro, I was imagining Milan play. Only Milan. No other team. The red and the black. No other colours.

Inter were a great team, but in those days Milan could call on players like Marco van Basten, Paolo Maldini, Franco Baresi. Absolute legends; champions whose level you could never reach, as I saw it. I spoke about them with Lysenko, who was an expert in all things Italian, loved beauty, and was a real maestro when it came to tactics.

Once it was over, we headed into town, admiring the Duomo from all the different corners of the square out in front. Up top, we saw the Madonnina statue, the great protector of the city: always stern, but ready to defend her place and watch over her people.

Lunch was served in a restaurant in the Vittorio Emanuele Gallery, the part of Milan which links the Duomo to La Scala. Under normal circumstances, we could never have afforded it, but the owner – another of Lysenko's friends – welcomed us as if we were family.

Before we went back to base to prepare for the last few matches of the tournament, we stood in front of the Sforzesco Castle and an enormous fountain. It's said that if you throw a coin in there, you will return one day.

I asked to borrow a coin. As I threw it in, I thought of San Siro.

HER NAME WAS UKRAINE

IT TOOK me only a few months – rather than the 12 established at our meeting – to convince my father that football and I were, and would always remain, two halves of the same whole. He became an ever more ardent supporter of mine, alongside my mum and sister Elena. It was goodbye forever to the military school.

In the meantime, however, came another birth. A daughter who belonged to everyone. A long-awaited miracle. We had the same heart, the same blood, the same pure soul. She was contagious, splendid, pure and her name was Ukraine. The newly independent Ukraine.

We officially left the Soviet Union on August 24, 1991. That summer in Kashira, a city a couple of hours' drive south of Moscow, we played in and won an important national youth tournament. For us, it was the last title we would win at USSR level. A general collapse was around the corner; you could spy big changes on the horizon. It wasn't rare to see soldiers and armoured cars on the streets. Even to a kid who was not yet 15 and knew little about politics, it was clear that something major was about to happen.

During the night between August 18 and August 19, there was an attempted *coup d'état* to get rid of Mikhail Gorbachev, the leader of the Soviet Union. The world was turning in a new direction and, after August 24, Kyiv had a different face. There were flags everywhere; in the streets, draped on balconies. Yellow and blue in every direction you looked. A new pride.

We were emerging from economic crisis, from daily displays of intolerance, from people's unhappiness, from the Cold War. It was going to take time to rebuild and start over. It wasn't easy but it was necessary.

At every level of football, Ukrainian leagues came into being. I was growing up at the same pace as my country. It needed to make its way among the other nations, just like I did when it came to my opponents on the football field. In the Dynamo reserves, I scored 21 goals in 55 appearances, with 12 of these strikes coming in a single season, making me the team's top scorer.

Whenever we played at home, big crowds came to watch. Once, for a Ukrainian Cup match, there were 14,000 fans. We were playing Dnipro (not their reserves but the first team, who were fighting for the top-flight title). We won 3-1 in the first leg of the last 16, with me scoring a double. In that period, I was called up for three different national age-group teams, including the Under-23 side that was trying to qualify for the Barcelona Olympics. My salary went from 50 dollars a month to 150, which I considered a huge amount. It caused me some embarrassment when I compared it to what my parents earned. Above all, I wanted to show them I deserved it. The first-team coach began to take a look at me. Yozhef Sabo arrived in 1993, having been a much-loved Dynamo player back in the day. With them, he had won the Soviet championship four times and the USSR Cup twice. With the national team, he had claimed a bronze medal at the 1972 Olympic Games in Munich.

Not long after he took the job, Sabo gave me my first experience with the big boys. He took me to a pre-season camp in Norway. I felt like I had made contact with the floor above. They invited me up, opened the door and I went in. I immediately noticed that the players were different to the ones I was used to measuring myself against: quicker, better prepared, with superior technical quality. They could think and make decisions in a split second.

I needed to learn as quickly as possible. I spoke little and observed a lot. I coped well with the physical fatigue because I was enjoying getting to know a different culture of hard work. It drove me on. When this little parenthesis came to an end, I went back to the reserve team and continued scoring goals.

The real turning point arrived towards the end of 1994 when I began to get many more opportunities with the first team. So many important dates set close together on a calendar of pure happiness.

On November 2, Sabo called me up for a Champions League trip to Paris Saint-Germain. This was something totally new and that's exactly how I lived it, with all the emotion that comes with a moment that you have worked towards for so long but which is still a mystery.

I had just turned 18 when I first heard the music. *That* music. The pre-match hymn that every player dreams of listening to sooner or later in their career. I trembled and shook. The PSG side had players like David Ginola, Rai and Patrick M'Boma. Not to mention George Weah, who would soon be up front for Milan and go on to become the 25th president of Liberia. His goal gave the hosts a 1-0 win. I watched from the stands, but it was like I had started: it all felt crazy, I was officially part of a team playing in the most prestigious competition in European football.

November 5 was my first-team debut, against Hazovyk Komarne in the last 16 of the Ukrainian Cup. Three days later came my league debut, against Shakhtar in Donetsk. I came off the bench after 54 minutes to replace Mikheil Jishkariani. I wasn't too emotional, because in my mind I had long been clear that sooner or later I would feature at this level. I just knew it was going to happen.

On November 23, I got my first Champions League minutes against Spartak in Moscow. On December 1, I scored my first league goal, against Dnipro. Six days later, I scored my first Champions League goal, in front of 25,000 fans in our own stadium against a Bayern Munich team coached by Giovanni Trapattoni.

On March 25, 1995, I made my Ukraine debut in a Euro 96 qualifier against Croatia in Zagreb. Four days later, destiny launched another signal. I found myself in front of Paolo Maldini, the biggest *Milanista* of them all. We were face-to-face, matching one another stride for stride. My second Ukraine cap came in Kyiv against an Italy team coached by Arrigo Sacchi. Our coach, Anatolij Konkov, opted for a 4-3-3, with me on the right side of the front three. This often put me on a collision course with Paolo.

I was young, very quick and well aware of my potential, but that game took away some of my certainty. After only a few minutes, I was asking myself: *How do I get past this guy?* I couldn't hold onto the ball without him gluing himself to me. He slid in, attacked me, targeted me, slung in crosses. Thanks to that encounter I really grew. Every blow to my certainty gave me another reason to improve.

We lost 2-0, with Attilio Lombardo and Gianfranco Zola both scoring. From that day on, whether in training or in a match, every time a defender tried to take the ball off me I imagined he was Maldini. Trying to reach his level became a positive obsession for me.

With Sabo, and during the brief tenures of Mykola Pavlov and Onyshchenko, I won the league and Ukrainian Cup at Dynamo. In my head, Sabo was also Maldini, because he too would not let me escape. Now and then, I went out at night with my friends, perhaps to a disco in Kyiv. We weren't doing anything wrong, but we were never alone. Sabo would have us followed and watched – a truly asphyxiating style of marking.

The nightclub bouncers in Kyiv had a terrible habit: if they saw players coming in, they would first phone our president's bodyguards and then the coach himself directly.

Sabo's interest in forgiveness was close to zero. He wanted to know every detail of our movements. We felt his breath on our collar and if the leash got too long, he would yank it – and us – back. Back in your beds, boys.

Sabo was our human shield against dangers of every size and type, including those on the road. When you turned 18, you were allowed to drive, and so I bought a car a few months before my birthday. Ahead of time, you might say.

It was a red Lada 2109 and so I didn't go unnoticed. I had a need for speed and so I got behind the wheel before I was allowed, which Sabo didn't like. So many arguments, so many rebukes!

He was a very emotional guy when it came to matters on the pitch as well. Always acting on instinct, he would shout in our faces. Pavlov was a calmer, milder fellow; the complete opposite of Sabo in his approach to handling the team. He helped me grow up and we built a lasting relationship. I have always considered him a 'pure' person with healthy principles.

At the start of my time in the first team, Sabo (who at one point was also coaching the national team alongside his club commitments), Pavlov and Onyshchenko all had stints in the dugout. The record books show: Sabo from January 7 1994 to December 1994. Onyshchenko from December 1994 to April 1995. Pavlov from April 1995 to June 1995. Then Sabo again from July 1995 to December 1996.

It was a downhill slalom from one person to another, each totally different. I lived it alongside Serhiy Rebrov, my perfect partner in attack. I had already met this gold-standard human being in the Olympic team. Being two years older than me, he played a crucial role in helping me establish myself in the group.

He, too, had started playing at a high level when he was still very young, so he understood perfectly how I was thinking and the difficulties I was experiencing. He gathered up and addressed the questions I had in my head but had not yet asked. We became friends and our on-pitch understanding was self-evident.

That wasn't the case immediately, however, because I was too much of an individual – an egotistical kind of player. I wanted to show people just how good I was. Serhiy explained to me that I was damaging the team, that I would be better served adapting my game to that of my colleagues. That on certain occasions, it was better to opt for one more pass and one fewer shot at goal.

I listened to him and followed his advice, and soon we

began to understand one another perfectly on the field. It was almost as if we had been created to complement one another. His movement was excellent, he always knew where I was and we saw the game in the same way.

When we were in camp, I would go to see him in his room. It was like entering a scientist's secret laboratory or the private study of an explorer. There were curious gadgets, contraptions and antennae everywhere you looked, as well as buttons, levers and maps.

Serhiy never slept. He was an amateur radio operator, one of those people who make contact with strangers across the world. When he finished training, Rebrov would eat, then head up to his room, where he stopped speaking his own language and started using English, in order to communicate with like-minded souls.

It was an intensive activity, which took up most of his nights. He rested only a little and still scored loads, which showed that it worked for him, not least because his hobby helped him cancel out the stress of playing matches.

He would tell us about picking up voices from the space station or the North Pole. Over the years, he would go on to win international renown for his radio work. It is even said that he once managed to establish 5,500 different lines of communication in the space of 48 hours. He knew everyone without really knowing anyone. He could chat away with the whole world from his room in the Dynamo team hotel, often with me by his side.

He would put on his headphones and immerse himself in a parallel dimension: one that opened up different stories, new interlocutors. Not everyone has Serhiy's capacity to get involved, not least when it came to choosing the right topics to discuss with those voices which were always new. He knew how to break the ice. To him, it was simply a question of character, of frequency, of passion.

On the pitch, meanwhile, his wavelength was always exactly the same as mine. We understood each other so well – all it took was a glance.

I don't know if Serhiy somehow managed to pick up any signals from the Kuwaiti Football Federation, but either way, at a certain point their manager resigned and became our new coach. He was known as The Colonel.

THE COLONEL

Valerij Lobanovsky had served in the MVD, the police force of the Russian interior ministry. He wasn't known as the Colonel by chance.

Out there on the football field, I was his faithful soldier. He shocked me to the point I was bewitched. He was everything for me. A very intense kind of everything.

I took orders and carried them out. I worked hard, grew and got better. I went to war in his name, battling until I had no sweat left to give. I was happy to get covered in mud, because there has never been a path to glory that wasn't a bit dirty or that didn't go uphill.

He preached sacrifice and reaping what you sow. His training sessions were resistance tests taken to the ultimate extreme; taken to the point where you were utterly exhausted. When the last muscle was begging for mercy, when you were on the point of dying, you rose again. He equipped you with the power of sporting immortality.

The Colonel had coached Dynamo from 1973 to 1982 and then again from 1984 to 1990, winning two Cup Winners' Cups and helping Oleh Blokhin claim the 1975 Ballon d'Or. As a sign of thanks and recognition, the club had always kept his stadium office. As such, when he came back, he was coming home.

It happened officially on January 1, 1997, when he was announced as the team's new coach. In truth, he had been back in the job for a number of weeks. Towards the end of 1996, he had held one-to-one meetings with all the players, me included. That was the first time I had met him in person. I already knew a lot about him, but only through second-hand accounts that often drifted into adoration and hagiography.

"Andriy, come here, I need to talk to you."

The last few months of 1996 had been difficult for me because of an injury that I had suffered in Vienna on August 7. Five hours before the first leg of a Champions League qualifier against Rapid, I hurt myself in the team hotel. Getting out of bed, I slipped on the TV remote. It was a stupid little error with very serious consequences: I had torn my meniscus.

I couldn't get on my feet without help and my knee had swollen. Somehow, I still managed to get to the Ernst Happel Stadium to see us lose 2-0. I didn't take it well: I wanted to be playing, scoring, helping my teammates. I flipped between disappointment and anger to the point that I was having to cope with the pain produced by my thoughts as well as the knee itself.

That same night we flew back to Kyiv, where I was taken straight to a hospital for surgery. The first of my career. The following day, my parents came to visit and found me depressed. All I could see was darkness. Each time I tried to return, I was forced to overcome setbacks both big and small. That November, Sabo – who had taken the Ukraine job while he waited for Dynamo to announce that they were replacing him with Lobanovsky – called me up for a World Cup qualifier in Porto. The flight took four hours. At take-off, I was pretty much fully fit, but by the time we landed, my knee had filled with fluid. The latest disappointment in a difficult year. I flew back to Kyiv.

"Andriy, how are you?"

"Getting better, Valerij Vasilevic."

When you spoke to Lobanovsky, that's what you needed to call him, adding the patronym to his first name to show the link between him and his father. It was a form of respect. His office was basic and unadorned, which mirrored his personality. The only contents were a few trophies dotted around the room, a whiteboard covered in tactical designs and a desk weighed down by papers. When we met, he sat down almost immediately and so I did the same, facing him.

"Andriy, I've watched you play. You have quality and real potential to grow, but you need to be more alert on the pitch. You need to be ready both mentally and physically to be part of my Dynamo. You must dedicate every part of your being to football and the desire to get better. Think of others, not just yourself. I believe in you, but I expect discipline."

That phrase brought to mind Shpakov, the first coach who had spoken to me in those terms.

"Thank you, Valerij Vasilevic."

He didn't speak much but utilised the right concepts. He got straight to the point and fired me up before his training sessions drained me. They were truly exhausting. Our first camp was due to take place in Germany, and in the 10 days before we set off, we got to work in Kyiv with daily double sessions.

In the morning, we would meet at the training centre to be divided into two groups. The first would go running outside, where the temperature was 10 degrees below zero. The second would stay inside to do aerobics. We were stunned into silence: how could it be that a football team was doing aerobics lessons? The session would last 40 minutes, with no breaks and the music at full volume, at which point the two groups would swap.

In the afternoon, meanwhile, a ball would appear. The intensity would go up a further notch and nobody said a thing. Often, we would undertake physical tests, doing four lots of 400m followed by five lots of 300m. Run, run again, and then run again, with intervals and variation. In Germany, the doses actually increased. We were doing three sessions a day for a month – a real military programme.

The alarm went off at 6.45am. At 7am, you went to run for 45 minutes or made your way to the gym, where the conditioning coach would have set up various stations. You would do one for 30 seconds, rest for 30 seconds then move on to the next. A real *Via Crucis*, with us carrying the cross. An assembly line where the finished product was Dynamo Kyiv.

Breakfast was served at 10am. At 10.30am, Lobanovsky would be waiting for us out on the pitch for our first football session of the day, which was followed by a shower and a rest.

At 4pm, the alarm went off again and we would do ball work for a further two hours. Then it was shower, dinner, massage and back to our rooms. When we threw ourselves down on the beds, we were all destroyed. Except Rebrov, who would begin to bustle about with his radio gear.

Our coach was exceptionally tough. He introduced crazy training loads and would not stand even the slightest drop-off in tension or care. He was supported by various underlings, who would follow us around without missing a beat. He demanded the best from us: the more tired he thought we were, the harder he insisted we work.

Lobanovsky considered dribbling to be a fundamental part of the game, and as such he was always setting up one-v-one exercises. A player had to keep control of the ball and get past the other, who in turn was attempting to dispossess him.

He was a true revolutionary, the first to use a computer. Together with Anatolij Zelentsov, of the Dnipropetrovsk Institute of Physical Science, he developed a programme that could analyse games and calculate the movement of each individual player.

He had us doing everything: running with the ball, running without the ball, jumps, various devilish ideas that he himself had come up with. And this is not to mention the so-called death climb: a track with a 16% incline which we had to go up and down an unspecified number of times. Just about everyone threw up before the end, but I never did. If you weren't sick, you would be given a starter's jersey for the matches. If everyone threw up, the starters would be those who had done so the least. It never crossed my mind to give up; the sheer hardship of those moments stimulated me. I loved pushing myself. It was something that I needed.

Lobanovsky was inflexible. He read philosophical works and said on repeat that without training, there would be no happy tomorrow. Those who never met him don't know what they missed. A genius. A visionary. A subversive perpetually on the trail of perfection. Someone who demolished the past and invented the time machine.

I witnessed experienced players crying at his feet, begging him to call off the session early. He always refused. In my very own timeline, he is ground zero. There is the time before-Lobanovsky and the time after. A reference point, my compass, my religion. The psychologist who fortified my mind, the guy who stopped me smoking, the terrain that allowed me to put down roots and grow both in terms of credibility and stability.

After the camp in Germany, we did another in Israel, with absolutely no drop-off in intensity. Under his command, we immediately won the league with four games still to play. We were 11 points clear of Shakhtar Donetsk at that point. In the final rounds of the championship, I felt some pain in my knee – the other one, not the one I'd had surgery on in 1996 – and it was determined that I required a small cartilage clean-up operation.

Between the end of the season and the start of the following one, there was precious little time. Before they knew it, my teammates were heading off for another 10-day camp, this time in Yalta in Crimea, which was still a Ukrainian city to all intents and purposes until the Russian invasion of 2014.

I stayed behind in Kyiv to do my rehabilitation. When everyone else came back, I felt better. Lobanovsky called me into his office and said: "Andriy, from now on I'm giving you a personal doctor and trainer, just for you. Here's a schedule – if you want to get back into the group, follow it with great care."

I read the schedule. It was practically identical to the one that had been given to my teammates in Yalta. There was only one difference: I had three days fewer in which to complete the work.

At the end of the allotted period, a test was arranged to see whether I was ready. I had to run the 300 metres to the stadium five times, with three minutes of rest between each shuttle. The target time was pretty modest and I managed to pass the test. My knee held up, but those last 300 metres felt like the Green Mile, the last walk undertaken by those on Death Row. Full of fire and fatigue, I could feel myself burning up. I moved forward by sheer force of will.

I gave everything and something more. The lesson, just the latest that I had learned, was clear: when you think you are coming towards the end, in reality you're experiencing a new beginning.

The Colonel was waiting for me at the end of the straight. "Andriy, tomorrow you can go back to training with the others."

"Thank you, Valerij Vasilevic."

I used the little breath I had left to pronounce his name correctly. That was always worth it.

A CAMP NOU HAT-TRICK

I F LOBANOVSKY had been a gift – and in a certain sense that's exactly what he was – he would have been a crystal ball. As soon as I looked within that incredible man, I saw the future and understood that he was going to change my life. All I had to do was listen to and follow him. If I managed that, the doors of football paradise would be flung open to me. And that's exactly how it went.

I immediately resolved that I would only leave Dynamo for a top European club, and in the meantime, I was going to work to get there. I started training with the team again in July but was still forced to sit out the first Champions League qualifier against the Welsh side Barry Town, whom we defeated without much fuss. It was then that the coach called me.

"Andriy, I think you're ready. How do you feel?"

"I feel good, Valerij Vasilevic."

"In that case, you're going to play."

"Thank you, Valerij Vasilevic."

I returned to the pitch in August 1997, in our second and decisive Champions League qualifier against Brondby. In the first leg, I scored in a 4-2 win away from home. We lost the return match 1-0 but still qualified for the group stage. There was a seat for us at the top table, too.

I loved everything about that competition: the atmosphere, the competing clubs, the individual champions who made it their playground, the anthem, the buzz in the air, the history, the stories still to be written, the emotion. If you wanted to become truly great, you had to find a way of imposing yourself in the Champions League.

Furthermore, Dynamo had the extra motivation of seeking revenge, of trying to rise again, after the one-year ban handed out by UEFA in 1995 for a failed attempt to bribe the referee ahead of a match against Panathinaikos.

It was on Champions League nights that I measured myself and my progress. The lights came on and the dance began. Alongside us in Group C were Barcelona, Newcastle and PSV Eindhoven. We set out with a label on our backs that we couldn't see but many experts insisted was there: sacrificial lambs.

Not a bit of it. Our first game was in the Netherlands, against Dick Advocaat's PSV. We won 3-1 and I got on the scoresheet. One of our opponents was Jaap Stam, and I just couldn't get my head around a defender being so physically imposing. He was massive, a true giant, and yet I managed to score a lovely goal in the 90th minute. On the turn, from outside the box at the back post, with an assist from Dmytro Mykhaylenko. I had on the No.10 shirt.

The next game brought Newcastle to our place, and both myself and Rebrov found the back of the net. We were 2-0 up at half-time but allowed ourselves to be pulled back to 2-2. Serhiy and I both created other opportunities to guide Dynamo to a win but when I had the ball at my feet, I wouldn't pass it to him, and he behaved in the same way towards me. We were like bickering twins.

We were late coming out of the dressing room after the match and got in the same car to head to a restaurant. Not long into the journey, Rebrov broke our silence.

"Tonight, Andriy, if we had passed each other the ball, we'd have won that game."

He was driving and had his hands gripped firmly on the wheel, but out of the corner of his eye he was watching me, waiting for my reaction in the passenger seat.

"You're right, Serhiy."

"Andriy, we mustn't be egotistical. We can't do that ever again. It's something we had already discussed. I'm sorry."

"I'm sorry, too."

We were moving slowly, trying to make our way through the crowds. All around was an infinite mass of men, women and children. It was late at night and they were heading home on foot. The metro simply couldn't cope with this number of people. A hundred thousand of them had turned out and in that precise moment, they all seemed to be right there, in front of our car.

"Andriy, do you see how many fans there are?"

"Absolutely incredible."

"We could have given them great joy. By the way, did you notice that they all seem happy?"

I hadn't noticed. We hadn't managed to beat Newcastle, yet our fans were still happy. They believed in us and came to watch us with pride. They followed us, they spurred us on and they had fun. They deserved better than two selfish friends. "Never again, Andriy."

"Never again, Serhiy."

Our iron pact was sealed there and then. It made us stronger and better and the same went for our teammates. The ones who paid the price were Louis van Gaal's Barcelona, whom we faced twice between October 22 and November 5, 1997.

In Kyiv, we outclassed them, even though their teamsheet featured names like Luis Figo, Rivaldo and Luis Enrique. We won 3-0, with goals from Rebrov, Maximov and Kalitvintsev. I hit the post.

We pressed like madmen and started to reap the rewards of another of Lobanovsky's tactical intuitions. He had taken Andrey Husin – who I had played up front with in the reserves – and put him in front of the defence. He went on to become a key figure in the group. Sadly, Andrey died aged just 41 in a motorcycle accident.

Rebrov and I had rediscovered our affinity. We felt like our coach's musketeers: one for all and all for one.

The city went crazy. All of Kyiv came out into the streets to celebrate for two days, while the players were holed up in a bar. Lots of the lads sang karaoke, but I didn't take the mic.

And what music the maestro, Valerij Vasilevic, was producing. We had transformed Dynamo into a strong, compact, aggressive, counter-attacking team. We spent so much time in camp and never complained. When we weren't training, we liked to distract ourselves by playing cards.

The best was yet to come. We were going to play at Camp Nou. Our morale was sky-high and when I woke up on the day of the game, I had an excellent feeling. I looked out the window of my hotel room and saw a cloudless sky. The sunshine augured well. The perfect canvas on which to paint some magic. We left the hotel to go through our final pre-match session and the temperature was close to 20°C. Back in Kyiv, it was a miracle if it reached 5°C at that time of year. It felt like spring deep inside each one of us.

When I stepped inside Camp Nou, everything seemed so big, but I wasn't afraid. Lobanovsky didn't say much before the game and on that occasion in particular, his silence was sacred.

In the ninth minute, we went 1-0 up thanks to my header.

In the 32nd minute, we went 2-0 up with another header from me.

In the 44th minute, we went 3-0 up when I scored a penalty that had been given for a foul on me.

A first-half hat-trick in one of the game's great temples, at 21 years old. The second half brought a fourth goal, this time scored by Rebrov. Thank heavens for the bridge we had built between us back in Kyiv.

In the dressing room at full-time, Lobanovsky came over to me.

"This is just the beginning, Andriy. You're reaching a level that only a few attain. Don't stop, don't ever get satisfied."

"Grazie, Valerij Vasilevic."

I then started to speak to myself, like madmen do. And, truth be told, I was indeed crazy with joy. I told myself one thing in particular: *You'll remember what's just happened for the rest of your life. It was your shop window, your big chance. Your night at La Scala. An unimaginable performance.*

Outside the stadium, the Barcelona fans gave us a sincere round of applause. I consider that on a level with my hat-trick as the most beautiful image of the night. They respected us. When we got back to Kyiv, we were greeted as returning heroes. Everything had changed for me. I now had a mobile phone and it began to ring incessantly. Agents were coming out of the woodwork from all sides, wanting to represent me, promising me the moon.

"I'll get you to Juventus."

"Well, I'll get you to Real Madrid."

"No, come with me to Bayern Munich."

They seemed to be in a competition to see who could give it the biggest talk, and I said no to them all. It wasn't yet time for me to leave the place I considered home. I didn't want for anything, but I still found it pleasing that people were talking about me. Moreover, I had only just introduced myself to the world: *Pleased to meet you, my name is Andriy and I play football.* I was living proof that the wind could blow from the east as well.

In the last two games of our section, we drew 1-1 with PSV in Kyiv and lost 2-0 to Newcastle at St James' Park. That result had no bearing on our qualification for the quarter-finals, where we would play a Juventus team coached by Marcello Lippi.

We'd talk about the Champions League again after the winter break, or, more precisely, at the end of another camp in Israel. Theoretically, it was designed to recharge our batteries before the second half of the season, but in reality, it was required to fulfil the exhausting schedule of work drawn up by the Colonel.

Lobanovsky wasn't well at that time, and so he followed the sessions from the window of his room on the third floor of the hotel, which had a direct view of the pitch. He was commanding from on high.

Some days, the schedule began with a 200-metre run without the ball. Then 400 metres. Then 600. Then 800. Then 1000. One distance after the other at elevated speed. We were preparing for the Olympics without actually being participants. In the meantime, I began to notice the pitch-side presence of a man I'd never seen before. Day after day, he was always there. He seemed to have a particular focus on me and my work. He would discreetly scrutinise every move I made. Then, at the end of every session, he would simply disappear.

One day I waited for him in front of the lift. I let all my teammates go in front of me and then in the distance I saw him approaching. He was headed straight for me. When we were face to face, he said: "Hello Andriy. I know everything about you. I need to go back to Italy right now, but we will meet again."

I didn't reply, partly out of shyness but for the most part because I was so taken aback. No sooner was he there than he was gone, shrouded in an air of mystery.

His name was Rezo Chokhonelidze. He worked for Milan.

HE IS A MILAN PLAYER

WHEN the team returned from Israel, I started seeing him everywhere. Whenever I trained with Dynamo Kyiv, he was there. When we played in Europe, he was there. When I was called up to the national team, he was there as well.

By that stage, having discovered his existence and memorised his features, I could gather proof of his presence. Discreet yet constant, he kept his distance but never abandoned me. He was like my well-aged shadow. An unexpected bodyguard. My pass to a goal I'd long been working towards.

I found out some details. Rezo was born in Tbilisi, which is now the capital of Georgia, on December 21, 1948. He had played in his home city for Dinamo and then, as captain, with Dynamo Leningrad. Twice in as many years he had been a European champion with the

Soviet Union Under-17s. He had been chosen to represent his country at the Olympics, but never got to step out on that stage because of a boycott.

In the 1980s, he enrolled in the Moscow Coaches School, where he studied football. As a player, he had been a handy left-back and now he was marking me. He had been tailing me – in a sporting sense – for 18 months without me realising. He had done an excellent job of respecting a deal struck between Dynamo Kyiv and Milan: he was allowed to follow me on behalf of the Italian club, anywhere and everywhere, but no direct contact with me was permitted.

He sent back thousands of reports to Milan which became legendary among the tight circle of people who knew of their existence. In the meantime, I too was becoming a little like Sherlock Holmes in my bid to know more, and my research was bearing fruit.

I found out about a report compiled by Italo Galbiati, who at that time was a Milan scout and would later become Fabio Capello's long-term lieutenant. He put it together after my hat-trick in Barcelona, sweet words battered out on an old typewriter.

This player is extremely strong physically. He is fast with or without the ball. He has real imagination and is genuinely two-footed. He scores goals and is strong in the air. He can play right across the frontline and knows how to get in behind like few others. Considering how young he is, I was taken aback by how easy he makes the game look. He is an emerging talent. It would be superfluous to add more. HE IS A MILAN PLAYER.

He had written the last few words exactly like that, in capital letters. Reading them, my focus on my day-to-day work remained intact while my self-esteem only grew.

When the Champions League resumed, we set off for Turin for the first leg of our quarter-final against Juventus. Rezo was the first person that I saw: he seemed to have a certain rapport with Lobanovsky (who by this stage was feeling better) and with Ihor and Hryhoriy Surkis, the brothers who owned Dynamo. They would meet up, chat, talk about this and that. All the pieces of the puzzle were falling into place, with all the protagonists merely waiting for the perfect solution. I had my part to play on the pitch, even if on that occasion, at the Stadio Delle Alpi, it was far from easy.

Our opponents had men like Inzaghi, Zidane and Del Piero. In defence, they had Montero and all those other guys who doubled up on me all night, right when I was about to receive the ball or in the split second after I got it.

I just couldn't get going. Lippi had worked out how to stop me – he has always been a master of his art. I was far from my best and we drew 1-1. The fact we were returning from our winter break did not help matters from a physical point of view, and in the second leg in Kyiv, things went from bad to worse. We lost 4-1, with Inzaghi scoring a hat-trick after we had kept them at 1-1 on the night until the 65th minute. We had been knocked out, while Juventus would only be stopped in the final, where they were beaten by Real Madrid and a single goal from Pedrag Mijatovic.

That disappointment did a lot for us, not least in giving us another push. To make strides in Europe, we would need to work even harder. With a man like Lobanovsky at the helm, there was no fear of the extra effort required.

That had long been our routine, one which took us to another league title and my second Ukrainian Cup in that same season, 1997/98. I scored 33 goals. My tally of 19 in the league put me second behind Rebrov, while in the cup I was top of the charts with eight. In the Champions League, I scored six times in 10 games. For the record, I added another three in the CIS Cup, a tournament contested by a number of teams who had won league titles in the former Soviet republics.

I won the CIS Cup three times with Dynamo Kyiv and it was thanks to that competition that I discovered Kakhaber Kaladze, a defender with Dinamo Tbilisi. In January 1998, he became a teammate and then a great friend.

The time for big decisions was fast approaching. In Italy, the newspapers had started to write about Milan's interest in me, and half the agents in Europe were still courting me as I finished an extremely short summer break.

At the start of season 1998/99, I requested and was granted a meeting with the Surkis brothers in the stadium offices. I have always had a great relationship with them and, given this mutual respect, we held a very sincere and frank conversation. I was the first to speak.

"I know Milan are following me, and that other teams are too."

"We'll stop you right there, Andriy. We want to keep you here for another year."

"And then?"

"If the right offer arrives from a big club, we'll let you know and then we'll sell you."

"I'm quite happy to stay. I enjoy it here as you know. It feels like home and I love Lobanovsky, but I'd like some certainty about my immediate future as well."

I was asking for a salary increase for my last 12 months at the club.

"No problem, Andriy. You will have the certainty you desire."

As well as increasing my wages, they gave me a Range Rover. I moved around the streets of Kyiv without paying too much attention to the speed limit. In theory, I could have driven it as far as Rome and Roma, another Italian club who wanted me.

Their coach was Zdenek Zeman, famous for his exceptionally hard training sessions – the runs up and down the stadium steps would have been a walk in the park for someone accustomed to living with the Colonel's methods. Roma's idea was for me to move to Italy immediately, but I had shaken hands with the Surkis brothers, guaranteeing that I would stay, and Lobanovsky had had his say too.

"It's early days yet – stay another year."

And so, I said no. At that moment, given the circumstances and the promises I had made, it was the only possible answer. The right thing to do.

Parma also came looking. Their then owner, the businessman Calisto Tanzi, had opened a factory in Ukraine and signing me was seen as a move with strategic benefit. Ajax, Manchester United and Juventus all made enquiries. I couldn't say yes, and anyway, I still had Milan in my head. They started to take up all my thoughts. Destiny cannot be changed or stopped – you just need to let it travel down the tracks that it has chosen. I just had to wait.

I had a new, unfamiliar problem to deal with at that time: the season was well underway and I just couldn't score. Not even by mistake. I was in a panic. This was a totally new situation for me, never mind the fact that we were seriously running the risk of not qualifying for the Champions League.

In the second and decisive round of qualifiers, we faced Sparta Prague. In the first leg, at home on August 12, 1998, we lost 1-0, while in the second two weeks later we managed to score only two minutes from the end, thanks to a Gabriel own goal. I got the ball and struck it, with Gabriel running alongside. The ball was about to reach the goalkeeper, it deflected off his teammate and went into the net.

It was great that we had scored, but not even that goal bore my name. I ran towards the corner flag and celebrated with a knee-slide, but I knew all too well who had touched the ball last. It was just a little piece of make-believe to boost my morale.

We went through on penalties, despite me missing from 12 yards as well. Luckily, Dmytrulin was successful with the decisive one. I remember the heat, the black sky, the storm clearly approaching on the horizon.

Right after the final whistle, the heavens opened. The next day, the Prague newspapers wrote that they were tears for their team's elimination. I wasn't crying, but this period of abstinence was starting to worry me. At the exact moment I had everyone on my tail, goals wanted nothing to do with me. Lobanovsky saw that I wasn't happy and invited me into his office for a heart-to-heart.

"Andriy, you need to stay calm. I can tell you're down, but you just need to focus. I have so much belief in you: this is your year."

"Thank you, Valerij Vasilevic."

I left the room. The great man's words had a healthy and soothing effect on me. My allergy in front of goal lasted barely a month and then it was gone. On the road to healing, the international calendar had placed a historic fixture: Ukraine v Russia, September 5, 1998, Euro 2000 qualifier. The first head-to-head since Ukraine had claimed its independence in 1991.

Kyiv was boiling over, and not just with positive thoughts and intentions. Resentment and pride, and then sport.

Us against them. 11 against 11. 50 million people against 150 million. The small guys and the big guys, or at least that's how it seemed.

We won 3-2. I didn't score that time either, but I played well. No problem. The crowd was 82,100 or rather 82,099 plus one: Ariedo Braida, Milan's sporting director. I'd had a tip-off that he was coming and so I was playing for Ukraine – and for him – against Russia. I tripled my efforts. After the game, once I was clear of the dressing room, I received a summons from the Dynamo hierarchy.

"Andriy, tomorrow morning come to our offices. There is a person who wants to meet you." It wasn't difficult to work out who that might be.

Up until that moment, I had never met one of the Milan directors. I went along to the meeting and found the Surkis brothers in the office along with Braida. Rezo was also there, for the very first time coming out into the open in front of me and formalising the role that he had been given.

As Rezo spoke good Italian, he translated the words of Braida, a most elegant gentleman with well-groomed hair.

"Dearest Andriy, Milan are keeping an eye on you. We're happy that you are continuing to work with Lobanovsky – we know him and rate both him and his methods highly. Congratulations, you were very good last night, and don't worry that you didn't manage to score.

"We will continue to watch you. Rezo's eyes will be ours. Ah, I brought you a gift…"

As he said these last words, he reached into a bag and pulled out a shirt – like a magician might pull a rabbit from a hat. Pure magic. A real plot twist.

It had red-and-black stripes and was utterly stylish, just like the man who had brought it there. From Italy. For me.

It sparkled, like the most precious gem. On the shoulders,

in gold lettering, was written 'Shevchenko'. My name. Beneath it, the No.10. It was my shirt. My Milan shirt.

All that was missing was the gift message. That had been given to me in person by Braida's words.

"Andriy, in this jersey you'll win the Ballon d'Or."

Everyone burst out laughing. I just smiled.

SHOULD WE SIGN REBROV INSTEAD OF SHEVCHENKO?

I DIDN'T put it on straight away. And I wasn't alone when I did. Two special people deserved to be with me at that moment. I wanted to share it with my parents, and see myself reflected in their faces. I wanted to get emotional while they did.

As soon as I could, I went to join them at home. I put on the Milan shirt with great care. I then called them through.

"Mum, Dad, I need to show you something. How does this look on me?"

The look on their faces told me everything I needed to know. Everything that was trapped inside me was writ large in those expressions: admiration, joy, pride. Mum told me I looked good. I'm not sure Dad said those same words but that's what he was thinking.

"These colours really suit me, right?"

The whole scene only lasted a few seconds, but in the precise instant when your life is about to change for the better, the certainty of time becomes a useless frill. The shivers last for seconds – you can't keep up with how fast they can travel, you just feel the emotion. You feel hot when it's cold. You feel cold when it's hot. Having Milan on your skin has that effect.

There were still no signed contracts or agreements between the two clubs, but that little act of courtesy towards me could not go unnoticed. Braida was letting me know that I would become one of them; I just had to be patient. Had that not been the case, the Surkis brothers would never have let him meet me.

"Mum, Dad – I'm giving this to you; look after it." The jersey of my dreams simply had to stay with them. They had protected me on my journey. They had escorted me to this point, walking on their tip-toes, without ever letting me out of their sights.

As it transpired, things returned to normal without too much hassle. Clearly there had been some kind of psychological blockage to get through, a weight that Lobanovsky's words had helped lift and that the meeting with Braida had destroyed once and for all.

I unblocked myself as I celebrated my 22nd birthday. I was born on September 29, 1976, and on September 30, 1998, I scored against Lens in the second round of fixtures in Champions League Group E. Panathinaikos and Arsenal were the other two teams in there with us.

We won the group and qualified for the quarter-finals. At a certain point in our campaign, I met Adriano Galliani – right-hand man of the Milan owner Silvio Berlusconi – for the first time. To be precise, it was on November 25, 1998. In a best-case scenario, the temperature was 10 degrees below freezing that night, but it felt considerably colder. Galliani watched the game up in the stands, beside

Braida, and wasn't particularly lucky: I played poorly.

We Dynamo boys were usually pretty indifferent to the frosty climate of our home country, but that night we trembled too. We went out onto the pitch wearing everything that was permitted, from gloves to tights. Our opponents, by contrast, didn't seem to feel the cold that seeped into our bones. Some of them even opted to play in short-sleeve shirts.

We started badly and went in 1-0 down at half-time. I was the first back in the dressing room where Lobanovsky gave us a very precise order: "Take everything off. Get rid of all those useless things you're wearing. Bin the tights – you're here to fight, not dance. You're too protected… you look weak and delicate."

His wish was our command and in the second 45 minutes we completely turned the game around. We did it with our bare legs, but above all thanks to a goal from Rebrov and an own goal from Angelos Basinas. My performance was a bit of a non-event.

At the end of the game, Galliani turned to Braida and asked a very precise question: "Ariedo, are you sure we should sign Shevchenko and not Rebrov?"

"Don't worry, boss. Andriy is a brilliant player."

Galliani trusted him. Had he based his decision purely on what he had seen against Panathinaikos, he probably would have chosen my strike partner. He also took ill on that visit, heading back to Italy with some kind of pneumonia. For Galliani, it had been the worst of trips, while for me it had been another little gain: another face put to a name in an album about a future that was becoming ever less theoretical.

Two weeks later, I scored as we beat Lens 3-1 away from home to seal our spot in the last eight. When we got back to

Kyiv, I requested a meeting with the president.

"You made a promise that when the right moment came, you would let me go. Well, Milan want me and I would like to go immediately. As such, I believe the right moment is now."

"Andriy, prepare a small suitcase and we'll see how it goes. In a few days, you'll be flying."

Not only did the president agree, he even arranged for me to travel to Milan in a private jet. We based ourselves at the Four Seasons in the city centre – a 15th-Century convent that had been converted into a luxury hotel. That's where my prayers were well and truly answered. Within 48 hours, I had undergone a medical and signed a pre-contract with Milan.

Rezo spoke up. "Andriy, Dynamo will sell you now but you have to stay with them until the end of this Champions League campaign."

President Surkis was next to speak. "I told you that the suitcase needed to be small."

Then came Galliani, by now restored to full health. "Welcome to Milan, Andriy."

The second last man to speak was Braida. "Remember: the shirt and the Ballon d'Or…"

Finally it was my turn. "Thank you. I'm signing with great joy, but in a year's time we will be sitting back around the table to discuss a contract extension."

I was that sure of myself. I started to imagine what my journey with that club could be like, and I wanted others to be able to picture it as well.

Galliani reassured me: "Andriy, we want you to spend a long time here too."

On the return flight, Surkis told me that our trip – to the very limit of what was possible – had to remain a secret. "You can't even tell your teammates," he said. "We know, Lobanovsky knows and that's it. Nobody else." "But of course. I'll only tell my parents." I gave them my draft contract to store alongside that Milan shirt.

I suddenly felt much freer, in my head and in my spirit. It was almost as if when handing me the pen to sign my pre-contract, they had also given me an eraser to rub out the rest of the pressure that had built up. I was happy.

In previous years, other players had arrived in Italy from Dynamo Kyiv. For example, Oleksiy Mykhaylychenko at Sampdoria and Oleksandr Zavarov at Juventus. They hadn't done badly but neither had they done particularly well. I was desperate to be the first one that people truly remembered.

When I got to Italy, I wanted to stay. I wanted to win, without ever having to rely on luck. In my journey towards Milan, it had never played a part. I had constructed my path with hard work, brick by brick, and then laid the tarmac, goal after goal.

I had listened to Lobanovsky. I had sweated and sweated. I had ran like a condemned man, always uphill.

Only people who fail to properly prepare need to rely on luck. It's a cardboard weapon for the last, desperate battle.

I never wanted luck. And I didn't need it either.

WE CAN WIN THIS THING

Iᶠ I had courted fortune, had I considered it in any way useful, perhaps the draw for the quarter-finals of the Champions League would not have given us the reigning champions, Real Madrid.

Leading up to those matches, we played several friendlies. One of them stood out: Milan at San Siro. Me against Milan. My present co-existing with my future. I was playing with my teammates, against my teammates. Two teams in one, one player for two.

On February 10, 1999, we beat the *Rossoneri* 2-1, with one of the goals coming from a Kaladze free-kick. He, too, would go on to play for Milan but couldn't have known it at the time.

Alessandro Costacurta, universally known as Billy, was glued to me from the first minute. And he never shut up. I couldn't understand everything he was saying in English, but I got the jist. It was stuff like: "When you come over here, we're going to kick you black and blue in training." Or: "Sheva, that's what they call you, right? Italian football is hard – it's nothing like what you're used to in Ukraine."

He would get touch-tight and start pushing me, and so I pulled out a couple of my trademark bursts, leaving him in my wake. Ukrainian football was hard too. He smiled and so did I – this was just his way of breaking the ice and welcoming me into the fold.

Surkis had informed me that I couldn't tell anyone about my footballing tomorrow, and yet in Milan they all seemed to know what was happening. It was an open secret. At the end of the game, I met the coach, Alberto Zaccheroni, for a couple of minutes. "I'm pleased you've signed. I'm here waiting for you." Paolo Maldini was next to speak to me: "Remember that Milan is a faith, a sacred passion." I felt really good.

The following day, we were back on the pitch for another practice match, a 1-1 draw with Monza on their home patch at the Stadio Brianteo, where Galliani had begun his career as a sporting director. Kaladze scored in that one too.

Never mind Costacurta and the Monza defenders, Lobanovsky was also determined to mark me closely on that Italian trip. He didn't want me doing any interviews – I was to keep my concentration levels high. As soon as we got back to Kyiv, after a single day of rest, he summoned me and Rebrov to his office.

"Lads, how's it going?"

"Good, Valerij Vasilevic."

"Before facing Milan, the rest of the team undertook a significant volume of work. You missed it."

"Yes, Valerij Vasilevic, that's because we had a couple of slight fitness issues."

"Understood, but everything is fine now, right?"

"Yes, Valerij Vasilevic."

"Well then, get to work. You need to catch up with the rest of your teammates."

He killed us for three days solid. I've never known tiredness like it. The others only had one light training session in the morning, while we were on heavy double sessions, working in the afternoon when the temperature dropped to -15°C.

Stopping was not permitted. For me in particular, the message was not to be thinking too much about Milan. We still had the task of making this a magical season and of honouring the Champions League. In the dressing room, we were convinced that we could go all the way, which meant beating Real Madrid against the odds.

The first leg was in the diary for March 3, 1999, in the Santiago Bernabeu. As the big day approached, it became clear that Lobanovsky wanted to start Kaladze, who was due to turn 21 on February 27, a few days before we flew to Spain.

As teammates, respecting the rather limited room for manoeuvre that we had in such situations, we pushed for that solution: we could see that the boy was ready. He barely said a word, but on the pitch he was note-perfect.

It was partly down to him that things went well in Spain, where we drew 1-1. I scored first and then Mijatovic equalised. I felt strong, and was beating my man with ease. It was different to the previous season: I was a better player, more complete.

It was my intention to leave an indelible mark, an eternal memory, in my last months at Dynamo. I'll never forget the conversations we had among the group in the bowels of the Bernabeu: "We can win this thing."

We won the return match in Kyiv 2-0, with me scoring

both goals. We played in our white strips – it was our turn to be Real Madrid that night as we killed off the defending champions.

Bayern Munich awaited us in the semi-finals, with the first leg at home. After 90 utterly crazy minutes, the scoreline stood at 3-3. The timing of the goals says it all:

1-0: me, 16 minutes
2-0: me again, 43 minutes
2-1: Tarnat, 45 minutes
3-1: Kosovskiy, 50 minutes
3-2: Effenberg, 78 minutes
3-3: Jancker, 88 minutes

We also hit the bar and missed another couple of big chances. In the last ten minutes, we dropped too deep. They took full advantage.

In the second leg in Munich's Olympic Stadium, we lost 1-0 to a Mario Basler goal. The big difference between the teams was the Germans' clinical edge. They took their big chances and we did not. We just weren't sufficiently clinical or cool-headed.

The defeat was a really big blow, and I hated seeing the expression on Lobanovsky's face; the wrinkles caused by his displeasure. Looking at him, I could tell just how much he had wanted to win that trophy.

It wasn't easy to accept what had happened. My heart was bleeding. We had given our all to give our coach a satisfaction that would have been thoroughly deserved. On an individual level, I had managed to score eight goals in that Champions League campaign; 10 if we count the preliminary rounds. I ended up joint-top scorer with Dwight Yorke, who played 27 minutes more than me for

Manchester United as they won the competition.

For the Colonel, the outcome remained an open wound. We made him smile a little by winning the league by nine points from Shakhtar Donetsk and lifting the Ukrainian Cup again. It was in that competition that I wore the Dynamo shirt for the final time (or at least that's how it seemed back then).

It happened on May 30, the day in which Kyiv celebrates itself. People gather in parks and squares, where concerts and shows are put on to mark the birth of the city. We, by contrast, came together in the Olimpiyskiy Stadium with 71,000 fans to beat Karpaty 3-0 in the final.

My parting gift was another two goals, and the fans gave me a great send-off. I didn't feel too blue, however, because I knew I would return often to Ukraine to play for the national team. Before I left, Lobanovsky wanted to meet me.

"My dear Andriy, you've made so much progress. You're ready to take the next step and play for Milan. As soon as you arrive, you need to speak to the manager and the conditioning coach to make them understand that you are used to an extremely high training load. You need to maintain that in Italy – it's absolutely fundamental. If you don't, your body will suffer and the consequences will be severe.

"You also need to know that what's happening to you right now in your career is only the beginning. Don't sit back. Don't become satisfied. Keep your level high. I believe in you. I know that you have the ability and the values to make great strides in the game. You can make history. I'll be watching: call me whenever you want."

We left each other with a long embrace – something that had never happened before. It was after our Champions

League campaign ended that Surkis sent for me. I went up to his office and found a group of people waiting for me around a table. I didn't know most of them.

Surkis said: "Andriy, these guys are from the secret service."

"The secret service?"

"Mr Shevchenko, part of our job is intercepting the phone calls of the most dangerous criminals and listening to what they are saying. In the last few weeks, we have heard unpleasant conversations. They have been speaking about a potential plan to kidnap you. From today onwards, you will have a security detail. There will always be two agents to accompany you, day and night, 24/7."

"But…"

"Mr Shevchenko, it's not up for discussion. This is for your safety."

The break-up of the Soviet Union had caused chaos in some corners of the 15 republics. Criminality had taken root, not only in Ukraine. They were robbing people in broad daylight, walking out of restaurants and hotels without paying, not to mention the abductions. Between them, the criminals had split up the cities into areas they each controlled and when they heard that I was moving abroad to a major club, it struck them that I might be worth a fortune in ransom money.

The security detail acted discreetly. Over the course of the day, I had four different armed officers at my side. They worked in two shifts, during games, training sessions and trips to away fixtures, too. At the outset, I was a bit scared, but I soon got used to it. My privacy suffered, but it was an acceptable sacrifice. Had it been necessary, they would have used those weapons to protect me. In reality, nothing bad ever happened, and I never had the feeling that it was going to. By the end, they had become big Dynamo fans and would celebrate wins with us in the dressing room. And then one day, while the season was still going, one of the four came up to me with news.

"We no longer perceive any imminent danger, so you won't need to be accompanied by the secret service. Thanks for the patience you have shown and safe travels to Italy when the time comes." I never saw them again, but that doesn't mean they stopped protecting me.

In any event, one person was still looking after me from close quarters: Rezo. It was he who organised all the details of my departure for Milan. "Andriy, I'll come too and stay with you for a while. I'll help you settle in. Mr Galliani called me to say he's expecting you as soon as possible. Get ready, because you'll need to start studying again."

ITALIAN LESSONS

I NEEDED to go back to school; that's what Milan had decided. Their agreement with Dynamo Kyiv stipulated that I would arrive in Italy two months before the start of the season, so that I could learn Italian. Galliani and Braida had been categorical with Rezo about this point: "Language is fundamental. We want Andriy to be able to use ours to speak to his teammates and the coach. He needs to adapt quickly."

That's how big clubs work. And so, after winning the Ukrainian Cup, I was on my way. From the early days of June 1999, I went every day to the Italian-Russian Cultural Association in Milan's Piazza Duomo to immerse myself in a subject I had never studied before.

I heard new terms and tried to memorise them. At the start, I could barely understand a word and thought it better to communicate with gestures.

Every day, I would cross one of the city's most iconic spots on foot, which was always crammed full of people and tourists. Nobody ever recognised me: apart from a few photos in the newspapers, they had no idea who I was. Only once did I hear a shout in the distance.

"Shevchenko! Shevchenko! You're Shevchenko, right?"

It was a man. Rezo went over to him out of curiosity. "And who are you?"

"I'm Albanian – I always watch the matches from the Ukrainian league on TV."

To accelerate my learning, Galliani had asked his daughter Micol to take me along when she and her friends went shopping, to a bar or even for a walk around the city streets. I was their silent shadow, physically present but not much more. It was like I was still playing against Panathinaikos: I watched them as they chatted but didn't react to anything. After three weeks, I got angry.

"Rezo, I don't understand a thing. I'm allergic to Italian."

"Andriy, that's not true."

"It is. When they go to a bar they say *un cappuccino per favore* (a cappuccino please) or *vorrei un caffe con un cucchiaino e mezzo di zucchero* (I'd like a coffee with one and a half teaspoons of sugar). When they've finished a meal in a restaurant, it's *mi scusi, posso avere il conto?* (Excuse me, can I have the bill?) If they go into a shop, they'll say *possiamo dare un'occhiata a questo vestito?* (can we have a look at this dress?). So you see, I just don't understand anything I hear."

"Andriy, do you not realise you just said everything to me in Italian?"

"Ah…"

Without me noticing, the strategy that the Milan directors had come up with was working as they had hoped. It was beginning to bear some early, still massively unripe fruit. I would parrot words whose meaning I perhaps did not yet know, but at least the musicality of the language was becoming familiar. That was a first and fundamental step towards getting over the threshold of rejection.

Like every self-respecting Italian school, there came a point when mine closed its doors for a long summer break. I headed off to Sardinia for the pre-meet that was to flow into Milan's pre-season camp ahead of the 1999/00 campaign. It was my baptism as a *Rossonero*. After having won a 16th Italian title and given the players a month and a half off, the club had called me and the other new recruits to this seaside retreat. Among the others was Rino Gattuso, who had arrived from Rangers in Scotland.

I made my first gaffe at the airport in Olbia, leaving my wallet on a bench. A policeman returned it to me.

"Excuse me, is this yours?"

"Yes, thank you."

I sat back down for a moment then got up and walked off again. Almost immediately, the policeman was back. He had something in his hand.

"Listen, you've forgotten your wallet again."

"Yes, thank you." I knew that to be polite, this was the way to respond. After a few seconds, keeping my head down, I wandered off again. I had a vague sense of shame... and the same policeman on my tail.

"Sir, are you taking the piss?"

I didn't understand that phrase. Rezo did, however. "Please forgive him, he's a bit disoriented."

I had left my wallet on the bench for a third time. It's said that in the happiest moments in life, we become kids again. And I was an absent-minded child.

From there, we reached Cala del Faro, a beautiful corner of the Costa Smeralda, where we met the physios, the doctors, and the conditioners, Paolo Baffoni and Daniele Tognaccini. It was to them that I delivered Lobanovsky's message, in a mix of faltering Italian, limping English and Ukrainian.

"The Colonel told me that I need to work loads."

Zaccheroni stopped by briefly to say hello, but in reality that time had been designed by the club to allow us to make first contact with our new environment and how things worked. We spent most of our days on the beach, and only a couple of hours on the pitch or in the gym, in nearby Liscia di Vacca.

In a strength test, I proved that I could shift 4.2 times my body weight during a jump. Tognaccini only told me this later, adding that a normal player will manage around three times while anything between 3.5 and 4 is considered excellent. My 4.2, therefore, was a gleaming photo that I ought to have glued onto my identity card.

When it came to the power test, meanwhile, I managed 95% of the maximum that a footballer can develop. That missing 5% annoyed me just a little.

We new recruits spent two weeks in Cala del Faro, where from time to time the old boys – the ones who had recently been crowned champions of Italy – popped in. They would hang around for a couple of days, do a little bit of work, then leave.

Immediately after the title win, Costacurta, Demetrio Albertini and Massimo Ambrosini had hired a yacht, which at that point was moored in Porto Cervo. One day, they asked me out on a trip, which was really kind of them. They wanted to involve me, however the atmosphere soon risked turning embarrassing.

They spoke a lot and I understood very little. I spoke a little and they understood not a word. To save everyone from this hassle, as soon as we were out at sea, I took the jet-ski and headed off for a couple of hours. I was fleeing due to shyness.

I didn't go too far from the boat and every now and then I would raise my hand and signal 'ciao'. Poor soul, they must have thought.

The good news was that I was starting to think in Italian. Just a few words here and there in the Tower of Babel that my head was fast becoming. Little by little, I was adapting to my new surroundings. It wasn't easy, but I gave it my all because I knew that Galliani and Braida were right: it's just not feasible to have a team where the communication between everyone breaks down in the face of one man's hieroglyphics.

As if that message was not enough, it had been explained to me when I signed that Milan based a big part of its image on communication – in Italy, Europe and the wider world, as Berlusconi loved repeating. I had not yet met the president, but everyone told me he was rich. Very rich.

I was about to learn that he had loads of heart as well.

In this pre-camp period, I met all of my new teammates, but some of them only very briefly. Lots of them popped in for a little touch-up, a few unobtrusive tests, before heading back to enjoy their holiday.

When it came to my own relaxation, the president took care of everything. As usual, it was Rezo who told me the good news.

"Andriy, Berlusconi called. He says that it's too hot in Milan and so he's going to lend you one of his villas in Sardinia. He won't be there but he wants you to go there for a week."

"Will you be coming too?"

"Yes, don't worry, I'm not abandoning you."

"What if we went to a hotel instead?"

"Andriy…"

"Listen, Rezo, what if I have to chat to people when we're in the villa? I'm not capable yet."

"Don't worry; it will all be fine, you'll see."

I invited along a Ukrainian girl whom I was dating at the time. We were catapulted into a fairytale, a set from an Oscar-winning film, a little private city absolutely devoid of architectural defects. The attention to detail was obvious; nothing was left to chance.

I'd done well to listen to Rezo. Every now and then, I'd see something in that villa that took my breath away: I was in absolute wonder.

If I was hungry, chef Michele Persechini took care of it. If I wanted an Italian book, to absorb new concepts, there was a well-equipped library to hand. It was the sort of place you could easily imagine being photographed for a specialist magazine.

The paintings? All originals that belonged in a museum. This was a full-blown art gallery. If I wanted to swim in peace, I walked down to the sea via a private beach.

Football was catered for as well. I could practice my keepie-uppies – shoeless – on a pitch that was as good as anything you'd find at San Siro. The gardeners kept it gleaming at all times.

One day – I think it was the last one before I returned to Milan – a woman came up to me in somewhat timid fashion. Her face was marked by a few wrinkles in that way that makes women even more beautiful.

She worked in the villa.

"They tell me that your name is Andriy."

"Yes, thank you."

I paused. Rezo was on hand to help me with the

translation, which had been our established practice ever since that very first meeting with Braida in Kyiv.

"You don't know the president yet, but if you listen to him, you won't have any problems," she said. "He will become part of your family and you part of his. You'll discover his mindset and his generosity. He'll change you, for the better."

I was listening, not knowing where all this was going.

"My husband is one of the gardeners who tends the lawn. I wasn't well – they found a tumour in my breast, and when Berlusconi found out, he took care of me. He was generous beyond belief, beyond anything we were owed.

"He sent me to hospital and before my operation, he phoned me. 'You're in good hands,' he said. 'They're going to operate on you and save your life. You just need to be strong. We'll see each other soon.'

"Ten years later, I'm still here, and I was a nobody. Never betray the trust that he is giving you. Be loyal and everything will work out well, you'll see."

"Thank you, madam," I said as loudly as I could.

And thank you, Valerij Vasilevic. That part I only said to myself. I don't know why, but I immediately thought of Lobanovsky, hearing the woman's words.

And then I resumed my keepie-uppies.

SEVEN IN HEBREW IS SHEVA

THAT ball never hit the ground again. It flew along beside me. Me, who went back to Milan. Me, who went back to studying Italian in Duomo Square, where people began to properly recognise me.

Me, who on July 20, 1999, the first day of our pre-season camp, saw thousands of fans outside our training complex, Milanello. They were chanting my name, too.

Me, who the following night, at San Siro, wore that red-and-black shirt for the first time in a match. We played a 30-minute game in front of 50,000 people; a little family outing to celebrate the club's centenary.

On one side was Milan Gold and on the other was the team I was playing for, known as Milan Centenary. Guys like Abbiati, Sadotti, N'Gotty, Maldini, Gattuso, Albertini, De Ascentis, Tonetto, Ziege and Bierhoff were all alongside me. The other lot won, 1-0 thanks to a Ganz goal, but on this occasion the 'other lot' were still ours.

Zaccheroni went onto the pitch on a lunar roving vehicle driven by Eugene Cernan, the astronaut who had taken part in the Apollo 17 moon landings. It wasn't a time to be keeping your feet on the ground. Berlusconi had made us understand this in his own inimitable fashion.

Right in the middle of those centenary celebrations, I met him for the first time in person, at a party staged at the racecourse just beside the stadium. It was a fleeting introduction, in among hundreds of people and a few horses. I thanked him for his hospitality in Sardinia.

Of all the lines he threw out to the floor that night, I still remember this one: "I need to make a semi-official announcement to the team," he intoned. "I'm just about to cut the centenary cake but perhaps, if you don't win, I'll be using the same knife to cut off something else at the end of the season…"

Ah.

Joking aside, Milan were in a rebuild phase. While it's true that they had won the league the previous season, they had been knocked out in the quarter-finals of the Coppa Italia and, even more importantly, they hadn't been involved in the Champions League at all.

I had been top scorer in that tournament, which was one of the reasons why there was so much expectation on me. Speaking of high expectations, I must admit to putting them on Ambrosini, my room-mate at that camp. I immediately gave him a gift: an Italian-Ukrainian dictionary.

Up there in the Varese countryside where we were training, there was no sea nor jet-skis to hand and so I wouldn't be able to escape as I had done in Porto Cervo. And so I changed direction, opting for a solution that was less instinctive but more instructive. 'Pass me the remote control' was perhaps the most frequently translated phrase.

When I got up in the morning and opened the windows, still rubbing the sleep from my eyes, the first thing I saw was the main Milanello pitch. That woke me right up. Business and pleasure in a single image that really got the adrenaline pumping. That's what I lived for.

I had a freshly-minted number on my back. The No.10 belonged to Zvonimir Boban and I would never have dreamt of asking him for it. Indeed, I didn't want any of the numbers that were already taken and had told the club: 'You choose for me.'

Instead, one of my teammates, Ibrahim Ba, came to speak to me. "Andriy, I think you should take my No.7. It would be my pleasure to give it to you, because I believe it will bring you luck. I have a strong sensation that it will become magical for you."

Two days later, I took a phone call from a dear friend. He was in Israel and seemed strangely euphoric.

"Andriy, is it true that you've chosen the No.7 shirt?"

"Yes."

"Do you know how to say 'seven' in Hebrew?"

"No."

"'Seven' is 'Sheva'. That number is going to bring you loads of luck, I'm certain."

He was the second person to say that in the space of 48 hours.

Galliani, Braida and the whole club in general put us players in the perfect position to be able to think only of football. There was even a number you could call 24/7 to deal with any needs or emergencies. Milan was a special club, with special people.

Yet even though they treated us like sons, I didn't have a deep or complete sense of calm, because my dad had taken ill several months previously during a holiday to Cyprus.

He had suffered a heart attack and spent time recovering in a hospital on the island.

When the doctors gave him permission to fly back to Kyiv, it seemed like the situation was slowly getting better. But I knew him too well, knew that this forced stop in the long run would end up boring him. I was also well aware that he was unlikely to give up having a glass of good wine with his meals. The whole thing tormented me.

Ambrosini learned Ukrainian while I studied Italian. Once our Milanello camp was over, he often came to pick me up on his motorbike at the Jolly Hotel where I was staying in the centre of town. We would go out to dinner. With our helmets on, we passed by unnoticed.

Costacurta gave me a lift to training and on the way would teach me the Milanese dialect.

Everyone took care of me. Even Paolo Maldini. They pampered me, these champions who had climbed out of their posters just to give me a hand.

Zaccheroni – an exceptional man, intelligent coach and a true gentleman – did not put me under pressure. He explained with total clarity what we needed to do, and then he waited for me. In his head, he was picturing a Milan with a single striker and two men in behind. In Ukraine, I had always been free from fixed tactical plans, but over here things were different. It was like discovering a new, much more complicated world, one in which even those opponents who looked harmless on paper in reality turned up ultra-prepared and ready to fight.

I found that out straight away. On July 28 we played a friendly against Varese, who were down in Serie C1, the third tier of Italian football. We lost. They were a really organised side, coached by Mario Beretta. I said to myself: 'Wow, football really is hard here. I need to adapt without losing any time.' Looking back to that pre-season, I recall with fondness the game against Bayer Leverkusen at their place. I scored a double, but the thing I remember most is the connection I felt with the group, something that really pleased me. It was a feeling that needed to be fed every day, using the petrol and sweat I had in the tank. Always assuming I actually managed to get to Milanello for the sessions.

I had been given a company car – a fast one of the kind I have always liked. But in the first few weeks, I was scared to drive it, on account of not knowing the roads in Milan itself nor on the 30-mile journey from the Jolly Hotel to the training centre.

Every now and then, I ventured out at night in the desert created by the darkness, trying to get the measure of the city streets and the Milanese ring road. After all, Costacurta and Rezo would not be able to chauffeur me forever.

One morning, I said to myself: *Today I don't want any help. I'm going to drive myself to Milanello*.

It wasn't my best idea. Realising that I had not arrived, Rezo gave me a call.

"Andriy, is everything ok? I'm already here waiting for you."

"All good, Rezo. I'm just about there."

At least that's what I thought. After another hour, Rezo called again.

"Andriy, the session is about to start."

"Yes, yes, I told you: I'm just about there."

"I don't mean to stick my nose in your business, but can you tell me what's on the road signs? Read me what's written on the first one you see."

"Rezo, there's not a single one around here."

"Come on, read it."

"Verona, one mile."

"Andriy, I think you might have taken the wrong road…"

"No, Rezo, I'm just about there."

"Yes, Andriy. You'll get here, but just a tad late. Now turn around and come back."

I came off the motorway and re-entered in the opposite direction. I was really concentrating. After another indefinite amount of time, my phone went off again. It was Rezo.

"Andriy, you're just about here, right?"

"Yes, Rezo."

"Read me what's written on the first sign you see, please."

"No worries. There's a big green sign with a name on it."

"What name, Andriy?"

"Genoa."

Silence. Perhaps he had fainted. Luckily, that sign only indicated the direction of travel, rather than announcing the start of the city itself. Had I continued on that road, I would have reached the sea.

"Andriy, stay on the line, don't hang up."

Rezo quickly became my personal navigator. When I finally reached the gates of Milanello, someone gave a round of applause. It wasn't Zaccheroni, who did however forgive a mistake I had made in good faith.

To avoid any unpleasant misunderstandings, when Berlusconi invited me to Arcore for the first time not long after, I begged Rezo to drive. The president was waiting for me at the door of Villa San Martino, his residence in the green of Brianza between Milan and Lake Como. He was holding hands with a small boy.

"A very warm welcome, dear Andriy. This is little Luigi, one of my children. He wanted to meet you. Come on in. I'll show you my humble abode."

Galliani and Braida were already there.

"This is the park."

"This is the little church."

"This is the little football pitch."

"These are the flowers, which I personally take care of. I'm very attached to them."

The list went on and on. Every corner contained a surprise. As had been the case in Sardinia, what struck me most was the extreme attention to detail. It wasn't a case of beauty for its own sake. More than anything, it seemed like a refined way of thinking being brought to life.

Although I obviously didn't know Berlusconi well at that point, he gave me the impression of being a man who didn't stop at dreams, but took the next step of turning them into tangible reality.

"Did you know, Andriy, that to me you look like an angel?"

"An angel?"

"Yes, a little angel. You're blond, well-groomed, short hair, no beard. If only everyone was like that."

Angelo. I had never heard that word before. It sounded nice.

"You are an angel and Milan is the devil. That's the club nickname. Do you feel ready for the Italian league?"

"Yes, I'm ready."

"Serie A is a tough division. The defenders are the best in the world, you're going to have to work really hard. If you score 10 goals, you'll have done really well."

"No, Mr President. I'm going to score many more than 10."

"Ok, Ok." These words were said with a certain tenderness. Like when you're agreeing with a child who has just said something ridiculous.

Berlusconi resumed the conversation. "Let's do it like this, Andriy. If you score many more than 10, at the end of the season I'll lend you Villa Certosa in Sardinia, as well as a boat, for your summer holidays. You can bring whoever you want."

"Villa Certosa?"

"Yes, not the one where you've already been, in Porto Cervo. Another one, in Porto Rotondo. It's beautiful."

First league game, Lecce 2 Milan 2: goal

Second league game, Milan 3 Perugia 1: goal

Fifth league game, Lazio 4 Milan 4: hat-trick

By October 3, 1999, I had already reached half the target stipulated by Berlusconi just before he laid out the terms of our bet. At that point, there was a short international break and I went back to Kyiv to face Russia.

The game was set for October 9 in Moscow's Luzhniki Stadium, with a major part of our hopes of qualifying for Euro 2000 on the line. Russia and Ukraine on the same pitch again, and, once more, there was more than football going on.

I took advantage of being back to go see my father who, in the meantime, had been re-admitted to hospital. As I had feared would happen, he had taken ill again. Despite the doctors having expressly forbidden it, he had gone into the countryside to cut the grass. Not with a lawnmower, but some ridiculously heavy piece of kit that you had to roll from top to bottom using only your arms. It was far too much for his already struggling heart, which of course gave in again.

I asked to speak to the doctor responsible for his care. "Mr Shevchenko, I don't have good news for you. Your father's heart is damaged in two places and he needs absolute rest. We think we have everything we need here to help him."

I didn't waste a second. I called Milan, whom I had brought up to speed about the previous problems. The club immediately organised for my parents to be brought to Italy. As I was still living in a hotel, Milan helped me identify a house suitable for the three of us.

We ended up in a beautiful, spacious apartment on Via Marina, close to the Porta Venezia gardens. Rezo, Galliani and Braida contacted Professor Mario Vigano, a luminary of the world of heart surgery who worked out of the San Matteo hospital in nearby Pavia.

The doctors at the Kyiv hospital began to share my father's test results with their Italian colleague. I thought constantly about him and prayed that everything would be sorted soon. I knew that in his current condition it would be impossible to move him from his bed, never mind get him on a plane.

I went out to play Russia with my head full of other thoughts. Physically, I was in great shape, but my mind was elsewhere. There was already enough going on without the other issues which accompanied that match. Once again, it couldn't be considered a normal game, in a sporting sense or politically.

We arrived in Moscow to hostility and tension. The levels of both were so high that we were advised not to sleep in our hotel, and so we ended up spending the night in the Ukrainian embassy surrounded by the tightest security.

We didn't play well, and Russia went in front thanks to a free-kick from Valerij Karpin, who at that time played in midfield for Celta Vigo. Everyone will remember Vladimir Putin's celebration up in the stands.

Two minutes before the end, something happened which nobody in Ukraine – and probably Russia – will ever forget. A piece of play that wrote its way into history. We were awarded a free-kick, miles from goal and tight to our left-hand touchline. As I walked towards the ball, Sabo, our coach, was shouting like a madman from the dugout.

"What are you doing? Get out of there. Away! Don't shoot, get your backside into the box."

"Stay cool – I'm going to score."

I struck the ball. It went up, looking like it was headed straight for the sky. But suddenly it changed trajectory, moving towards the left and dropping slightly. It became an indecipherable parabola. Almost sweet, in its absolute murderous intent.

Filiminov, the goalkeeper, was caught unawares and had to take two steps back to attempt the save. He got both hands on the ball, but instead of simply parrying it clear, he knocked it into the net before ending up there himself. A surreal silence enveloped the stadium. Death had paid an unexpected visit: because of that 1-1 draw, Russia failed to qualify for the European Championships, while we progressed to a play-off against Slovenia. That's where it ended for us as well.

I threw myself back into my Milanese activities: football and preparing for the arrival of my parents. My new house was very peaceful, Costacurta and Ambrosini helped me move in the furniture and one afternoon Albertini rang the buzzer.

"Andriy, are you busy?"

"No, Demetrio, what's up?"

"I'll tell you after. In the meantime, get ready, because we need to go out."

Our destination was the supermarket.

"Andriy, it's simply not possible that you don't even know how to heat water to make pasta. We'll do some shopping then come back to yours for a quick-fire cooking course."

He liked me. I liked him. He made me laugh, and so did Serginho, a guy I loved to joke around with at training.

"Sergio, you're lazy, you need to work harder."

"No, Andriy, it's not me working too little, it's you working too hard."

One afternoon, the sun was shining beautifully over Milanello.

"Andriy, have you seen this brilliant weather?"

"Run, Sergio, run…"

"Andriy, in Brazil, sun means summer."

"Run!"

At that point, right in the middle of a small-sided training match between teammates, Serginho lay down on the pitch and closed his eyes.

"What on earth are you doing, Sergio?"

"Today it's summer, Andriy, and I'm enjoying the moment. Let me soak up the sun."

Serginho was able to make light of even serious situations – a precious gift. One laugh from him allowed you to tackle any moment with glee. *Toda joia, toda beleza.*

Dad finally obtained permission from the doctors to fly. When Professor Vigano operated on him, a quadruple bypass was required. I went to see him every day in Pavia, never once ending up on the wrong road. Mum never left his side: in times of pain, love really is forever.

Berlusconi made sure to keep himself up to speed. I began to count again, taking into account the games that I'd missed out while everything else had been going on.

Sixth league game, Milan 2 Cagliari 2: goal.

Seventh league game, Inter 1 Milan 2: goal, in my first derby, coming off the bench.

In the week leading up to that game, the *Gazzetta dello Sport* arranged a forum in their offices with the strikers from both teams. You had Vieri, Zamorano and Ronaldo on one side and Bierhoff and me on the other, as we waited for Weah to finally put in an appearance. He took forever, but when he did arrive, he was dressed from head to toe in military gear. It looked like he had just stepped out of a drill. Weah's message was clear: this is going to be a battle.

In truth, that description applied to the whole of that year's Serie A. There wasn't a clear favourite for the title – lots of teams could justifiably target such a success.

Thirteenth league game, Milan 2 Torino 0: goal.

At that point, however, our Champions League campaign was over before it had even really started. We finished bottom of Group H, behind Chelsea, Hertha Berlin and Galatasaray.

Fourteenth league game, Milan 2 Reggina 2: two goals.

Seventeenth league game, Udinese 1 Milan 2: goal.

At the half-way point in the season, I had scored 11 times. I met Berlusconi, who said: "Andriy, I already know how this will end up. I'm never making a bet with you again, else you take away even my trousers."

Nineteenth league game, Perugia 0 Milan 3: hat-trick. My second of the season.

Twentieth league game, Milan 4 Bari 1: goal.

Twenty-first league game, Bologna 2 Milan 3: goal.

Twenty-fourth league game, Milan 1 Inter 2: goal. The sight of the *Nerazzurri* inspired me; it was just a pity about the defeat.

Twenty-fifth league game, Milan 3 Verona 3: two goals.

Twenty-sixth league game, Milan 2 Juventus 0: two goals.

I wasn't scoring by chance. Ever since I arrived at Milan, I had understood that I would need to work really hard on my finishing if I was to get the better of the defenders in that league. For me, every training session lasted one hour longer than was scheduled. When the others went back into the Milanello dressing room for a shower, I stayed out with Valerio Fiori.

Showing great patience, he would go in goals while I took shots from every angle, on the run. My intention was to refine my technique but also to faithfully reproduce match situations. Fiori often repeated: "You're going to kill me with all these shots."

Thirty-first league game, Reggina 1 Milan 2: goal.

Thirty-third league game, Roma 1 Milan 1: goal.

At this point, there was only one game left in the league season. We were out of the title race but I was in the running for the top-scorer prize, the *Capocannoniere*. Udinese came to San Siro. Once again, my teammates showed themselves to be great people. They were trying to set me up to help me win the award. It finished 4-0 to us, with my name on the scoresheet. I'd done it.

As soon as I scored, I lifted up my head to see dozens of blue-and-yellow Ukraine flags in the stands. That moved me, especially when I considered how, back on the first day of the season, very few of these people would have known what and where Ukraine actually was.

I finished the season with 24 goals, one more than Fiorentina's Batistuta and two more than Hernan Crespo at Parma. After Michel Platini, I was only the second foreigner to have been top scorer in his first season in Serie A. Lazio won the *scudetto*, and Juventus finished second after their now famous rain-delayed defeat in Perugia. We came third.

A few days after the end of the season, Galliani called me into the old club offices in Via Turati.

"Andriy, do you still like cars?"

"Yes, always, Mr Galliani."

"Well, get yourself to the Mercedes garage and pick whichever one you want. You deserve it."

He increased my salary as well. When he signed my pre-contract, I had told him that one year later we would be discussing a renewal. When I signed the actual contract, I had said: "Money doesn't interest me. Above all, I want to show I'm worthy of Milan."

Dad was tired but improving.

Berlusconi kept his promise, giving me the keys to Villa Certosa. I invited Costacurta and one of our mutual friends, Piero Gaiardelli.

I enjoyed the rest. I was the top goalscorer in Serie A, but something was still worrying me: as a team, we hadn't managed to win anything. Regardless, the racecourse cake remained the only thing the president cut with that knife.

MADRID HAVE
MADE AN OFFER

I WAS learning to play like an Italian. To think like an Italian. To behave like an Italian. To move like an Italian. To go on holiday where the Italians went.

Even to feel Italian, from time to time – though I remained forever and proudly Ukrainian. In my head, heart and soul I was an ambassador for my brilliant homeland.

Two big things were missing for the transformation to be complete: I didn't eat like an Italian and I didn't dress like an Italian either.

Once again, it was Albertini who helped me out with the first issue. I was going out for dinner with all my teammates, and he particularly liked to take me to the Pomiroeu restaurant in Brianza, where the chef was Giancarlo Morelli. From a culinary perspective, I was born and raised in Albertini's arms, and through his recipes.

When I first arrived in Milan, I didn't like pasta and

didn't know of the existence of *pesce crudo* or dozens of other dishes. It is as if, over time, Albertini weaned me. First of all, he made me simple meals and then, when he considered me ready, he accompanied me to try new things, unknown flavours.

After my first taste of Milanese risotto, there was no going back, and the same went for the famous veal cutlets.

When it came to fashion, meanwhile, I ended up in seventh heaven. I met Giorgio Armani and became his friend. A great man of the world; an elegant man with elegant thoughts. They showed me his shop in town and I began to frequent it as a customer. Every which way I turned, I saw class and style.

I loved the clothes on display, I bought a few and then a whole load. The staff knew I was a footballer and treated me well. One day when I was in the shop, Leo Dell'Orco came in to meet me. He and Armani have long worked together, and he is a huge Milan fan. He's a lovely, kind, very open guy, and his whole manner made me like him immediately.

He started sending me clothes and one day he said, "Come on, let's go and meet Giorgio".

In his showroom, in the middle of his house, we shared a coffee. I was shy and so didn't say much on that occasion either. I think I must have uttered a phrase like, "you are a true genius".

After that, we met up for a few dinners, at Nobu and the Armani Caffe, both of which had just opened. Often Costacurta would come too. Sitting around a table or looking into a mirror are other ways in which you can get used to your surroundings.

Off the pitch, things were going well but it was a different story on it: season 2000/1 seemed cursed. I never stopped scoring, but as a team we ran into some problems.

In the league, we went through a December dip. In the Champions League, we qualified by beating Dinamo Zagreb, with me scoring four goals across the two legs, then made it through the first group phase, finishing ahead of Leeds, Barcelona and Besiktas. However, we were knocked out in the second phase, where a home draw with Deportivo La Coruna proved to be fatal.

Because of that result, midway through March 2001, Zaccheroni was sacked, which upset me a lot. I will never stop thanking him for how he treated me and the opportunities he gave me. Every memory I have of him is positive and affectionate.

Cesare Maldini and Mauro Tassotti were chosen to replace him until the end of the season. One was Paolo's father and had captained Milan to the 1963 European Cup at Wembley. The other, who was a teammate of Paolo, had retired in 1997 after playing more than 400 games in the red-and-black jersey and winning everything there was to win.

Tassotti-Maldini: it had a good ring to it. I had so much respect for the Maldini family, and Paolo called Cesare 'dad' not 'boss'. With our new coaching team, we managed to create a bit of history by beating Inter 6-0 on May 11, 2011. Among our starters that day was Kaladze, my former Dynamo Kyiv teammate whom Berlusconi had bought in January, after having asked me what I thought of him.

My response was straightforward: "I think he's worthy of Milan."

I scored twice in that game, as did Gianni Comandini. Federico Giunti and Serginho both found the back of the net as well, the latter having finally stopped soaking up the sun at Milanello. That day, he himself was the sun and we all looked that bit more beautiful.

We were fully aware that, in the space of 90 minutes, we were trying to give some kind of meaning to a season that until that point had lacked one.

6-0: Game. Set. Match.

A game of tennis, 11-a-side. I knew that my friend and countryman Andrei Medvedev would be proud of me. On those rare occasions when I got some time off, we would have a hit on the clay courts of the Monte Carlo Country Club. He put me up in his apartment until such time as I got one of my own.

Athletically, I could hold my own, but when it came to technique he outclassed me, winning by exaggerated margins. I would get angry, even though I knew that he had been No.4 in the world and a finalist at Roland Garros in 1999, when he lost in five memorable sets to Andre Agassi. I've always had a competitive spirit, regardless of the sporting discipline.

It was the same story whenever I played Boban, with whom I had remained friends after he left Milan in 2001. I thought I was pretty good, but it would always finish two sets to love to him. One time, I played him three days in a row. The first match finished 6-0, 6-1. I was running about like a madman while Zvone just laughed.

"Andriy, I think you need to improve."

That night, I went to bed with thoughts of beating him. I hardly got a wink of sleep all night. The following day, it was the same story: 6-0, 6-2.

"You see, Andriy? You won one game more. You're getting better."

Third day? Same story. There was nothing I could do, not least because he could call on the advice of an exceptional man like Goran Ivanisevic, who had been world No.2. Over the years, I lost often to Croatia's former world No.3

Ivan Ljubicic as well, so I cherish the memory of that 6-0 against Inter. Just one set, but of the highest quality.

Sadly, it didn't allow us to finish the season in a respectable position. We came sixth, 26 points behind the winners, Roma, with Juventus, Lazio, Parma and Inter all ahead of us too. We qualified for the following season's UEFA Cup.

And I said no to Real Madrid.

I knew they were watching me, even if nobody from the Spanish club had ever contacted me directly. The rumours were always there. With the Serie A season still ongoing, I received a call.

"Mr Shevchenko, good evening. I'm calling you from Arcore, I'm Mr Berlusconi's secretary. Can I pass you over?"

I was sitting on the sofa at home, watching TV. Instinctively, I grabbed the remote and switched it off.

"Certainly."

"Ciao, Andriy. I've got something to tell you."

"Good evening, Mr Berlusconi. I'm listening."

"Florentino Perez, the Real president, has made a very serious offer to take you to Madrid. I'll preface this by saying that the club has no intention of selling. Milan do not sell players. But I need to ask: are you going to leave us?"

When you are asked certain questions, there are only two options. You can take time to think it over or you can get straight to the point, knowing that the response is already there, just waiting to be pulled out when the situation arises.

I reckon many players would vacillate when faced with that kind of professional opportunity, but I knew exactly what I wanted. More than anything, I knew what I felt, and feelings have a specific weight that has to count for something when it comes to the biggest decisions. That's what I said to Berlusconi.

"Mr President, the offer you have received makes me

feel emotional. We are talking about Real Madrid, one of the most noble clubs in the world. However, no, I have no intention of leaving. I want to stay here with all my heart: I feel that my journey with this team is not yet finished."

"Good man, Andriy."

"I want to win the Champions League in a Milan shirt. Milan is my home."

"Excellent, Andriy. This is music to my ears."

"My Real Madrid is Milan."

"Thank you, Andriy. At the end of the season you will meet with Galliani to speak about sorting you a new contract. I wish you a pleasant evening."

It was very pleasant. I slept like a baby. Blissfully happy. I saw Real Madrid, Spanish champions, and Milan, sixth in Serie A – and I smiled. I read that Real Madrid had just reached the semi-finals of the Champions League, a competition that Milan had exited some time previously, and I smiled again. I knew that Real Madrid would be in the Champions League the following year as well, while Milan would be in the UEFA Cup. Another smile.

I pictured the Real Madrid dugout, occupied by the legendary Vicente Del Bosque, at the exact same time that nobody knew with any certainty who would be coming after Tassotti and Maldini. Yet another smile. Never a backwards step. Never a second thought. Just happiness and love for the colours that I wore.

Thank you Real Madrid, thank you so much – but long live Milan. And long live the 34 goals I had scored in all competitions that season.

As Berlusconi had said would be the case, before I went on holiday, Galliani called me into the club offices. The only item on the agenda was my wages. For the first time since we had known each other, we couldn't reach agreement on something. I knew exactly what I was worth, and thus how much to ask for, but the offer that was made fell well short of my request. I was left feeling hurt.

"Mr Galliani, I deserve more. Now you know what I'm thinking."

"Andriy, it wouldn't be right for me and you to argue. Let's do it this way: you focus on your holiday and try to detach yourself for a while. When you get back, we'll pick up the conversation."

I left for the Costa Azzurra, but I wasn't on my own. By my side was Kristen, a beautiful girl. We were always hand-in-hand.

Shevchenko's early years at Dynamo Kyiv instilled discipline and shielded him from the lawlessness which marked the demise of the Soviet Union. Trips to youth tournaments in Italy and Wales opened his eyes to a world beyond his home country and accelerated his progress to first-team football. *Andriy Shevchenko*

Shevchenko and Serhiy Rebrov formed
a prolific partnership for Dynamo Kyiv
and Ukraine. Off the pitch, they were
room-mates, and Rebrov would indulge
his passion as an amateur radio operator.
"He could chat away with the whole
world from his room in the Dynamo
team hotel, often with me by his side,"
said Shevchenko.

Reunited, right, at the Game4Ukraine
in August 2023.
Getty / United24

Carlo Ancelotti's arrival as Milan coach in November 2001 ushered in a period of incredible success for the club, including the 2003 Champions League – when Shevchenko scored the winning penalty. The pair's relationship, however, was occasionally stormy, and included fallouts over injuries and lack of game time. Ultimately, the mutual understanding which developed became a lifelong friendship. Ancelotti said: "We loved one another and still do, very much, but we have also had cross words, perhaps because of a virtue that we share: we always say what we think."

Imago

Shevchenko first faced Paolo Maldini in March 1995, when Ukraine lost 2-0 to an Arrigo Sacchi-coached Italy. "I was young, very quick and well aware of my potential, but that game took away some of my certainty. After only a few minutes, I was asking myself: *How do I get past this guy?*"

Later, at Milan, they became friends – and neighbours – with Shevchenko drawing from his more experienced teammate in times of high pressure. Of the build-up to the 2003 Champions League final, Shevchenko said: "Maldini was calm. Costacurta was serene. Both of them had already lifted the trophy three times and knew what was required. Seeing how they were gave us confidence and strength."

Imago

Shevchenko tries to dispossess Bayern Munich midfielder and World Cup winner Lothar Matthaus in one of the great Champions League semi-finals of all-time in April 1999. A breathless first leg in Kyiv finished 3-3, after the home side surrendered the lead three times. In the second leg, a Mario Basler goal was enough to deny a dazzling young Kyiv side – coached by the legendary Valerij Lobanovsky. "The defeat was a really big blow, and I hated seeing the expression on Lobanovsky's face; the wrinkles caused by his displeasure. Looking at him, I could tell just how much he had wanted to win that trophy… My heart was bleeding."

Imago

Kaka arrived at Milan after the 2003 Champions League win – and immediately established himself as a phenomenon. "Right from the very first training session, he left us open-mouthed. A 21-year-old Brazilian kid who did everything right."

Imago

Shevchenko's transition to Milan was eased by the presence of experienced senior pros like Paolo Maldini, Alessandro Costacurta and Demetrio Albertini, right. The latter decided one day that the young Ukrainian's cooking skills were not up to scratch. He told him: "Andriy, it's simply not possible that you don't even know how to heat water to make pasta. We'll do some shopping then come back to yours for a quick-fire cooking course."

Imago

When he failed the entry exam for Kyiv's University of Physical Education and Culture at 16, Shevchenko's parents, above, allowed him one year at Dynamo Kyiv to prove that football could be his future. If not, he would attend military school instead. "It took me only a few months – rather than the 12 established at our meeting – to convince my father that football and I were, and would always remain, two halves of the same whole... It was goodbye forever to the military school."

Andriy Shevchenko

Shevchenko with his mother, sister Elena and niece, above left. His mother and sister refused to leave their homeland after the 2022 Russian invasion; Shevchenko with his four sons, Jordan, Kristian, Alexander and Ryder.

Andriy Shevchenko

Valerij Lobanovsky was the biggest influence on Shevchenko's career. His revolutionary techniques combined with a fierce approach to physical conditioning transformed Shevchenko into one of the best young strikers in Europe – and paved his move from Dynamo Kyiv to Milan.

When the *Rossoneri* won the 2003 Champions League, Shevchenko brought the trophy back to Kyiv, where his mentor had passed away the year before. "I took the trophy to Lobanovsky's statue, outside the Dynamo stadium. Promises must be kept. The statue had him sitting on a bench, and so I slipped the trophy in there beside him. He deserved it – it was his."
Andriy Shevchenko

A move to Chelsea – after a long courtship from Roman Abramovich – failed to live up to expectations. Shevchenko's goal against Valencia in the second leg of the Champions League quarter-final in April 2007 – Chelsea won 3-2 on aggregate but went on to lose to Liverpool in the semi-final – was a rare high point. He found himself bedevilled by a succession of injuries and moved back to Milan on loan in season 2008/9.

Imago

The 2006 World Cup in Germany established Ukraine as a force in world football. After a heavy loss to Spain in their opening match, they beat Saudi Arabia and Tunisia before knocking out Switzerland in the last 16. A 3-0 loss to Italy in the quarter-finals failed to overshadow a remarkable tournament in their first World Cup as an independent nation. "When we returned to Kyiv, people came out into the streets to thank us. Ukraine had just become one of the top eight teams in the world, part of the footballing G8. Italy. France. Germany. Portugal. Brazil. Argentina. England. Us."

Imago

Milan's surrendering of a 3-0 lead to Liverpool in the 2005 Champions League final in Istanbul – and subsequent loss on penalties – was one of the darkest moments in the club's history and a personal devastation for Shevchenko, who had his penalty saved by Jerzy Dudek. He struggled to sleep for months afterwards, but gave Liverpool credit: "They had given everything. They had battled with their hearts. We simply could not have won that game."
Imago

In 2004, Shevchenko became the third Ukrainian in history to win the Ballon d'Or, after Oleh Blohkin in 1975 and Ihor Belanov in 1986. His 24 league goals carried Milan to the Serie A title and saw off competition from Deco and Ronaldinho.

The ceremony proved an unforgettable experience. "Berlusconi loaned me one of his private jets, a Falcon, for the flight to Paris. On the return journey, Galliani was euphoric and we had a photo taken (below) that to this day is close to both our hearts."

Imago / Andriy Shevchenko

His spell at Milan was a time of professional fulfilment for Shevchenko, but it was also the city where he met his wife, Kristen. "She was American. She didn't speak Italian well, and my English wasn't great, but we understood each other straight away."

Imago

Shevchenko struck the winning penalty to win the 2003 Champions League final for Milan against Juventus. "I ran my tongue over my bottom lip. It was dry. The run-up. The strike. Buffon moved to his right, I went to his left. Goal. 3-2. Milan, champions of Europe… I gave my first embrace to Dida… He was simply the first guy I came across on my mad run with no destination in mind."
Imago

In 2016, Shevchenko became the manager of Ukraine and led his country to Euro 2020, where they reached the quarter-finals for the first time in their history.

Imago

Russia's invasion of Ukraine in February 2022 changed everything for Shevchenko. His mother and sister chose to remain in the country, while Shevchenko began a diplomatic effort to raise money and awareness. "I was engaged by the Ukrainian president, Volodymyr Zelensky, a hero among heroes, a man who from the very first second of the war undertook not to abandon his people and his country. Just like my mum and sister."

United24

MY NAME IS KRISTEN

TALL, blonde, a living work of art. Just perfect. Simply: Kristen. The first time I saw her, a few months previously, Russell Crowe was singing in the background. The *Gladiator* star was not in Rome but Milan, having swapped the Colosseum for the amphitheatre of fashion.

A guest of Giorgio Armani for his shows at Milan Fashion Week, Crowe was performing with his band, *30 Odd Foot of Grunts,* on stage at the Rolling Stone Club during a charity night. I was also among the guests.

I was thirsty: there were lots of people around and I had started to feel hot. I ventured towards the bar with Ricky Toloi, a very well-known figure on the Milanese nightlife scene. And suddenly, there she was. So beautiful she took your breath away. Almost mysterious, as she stood there enveloped by the low-lighting in the disco. My heart skipped a beat and for a second, nothing made sense.

As I continued walking, our paths crossed and we looked

each other in the eye. It was just a glance, but long enough for me to know I would never forget her. As usual, to begin with I couldn't get a word out.

"Ciao, are you that Milan player?"

"Yes."

"I like how you're playing."

"Ah, thanks."

"My name is Kristen."

"I'm Andriy, pleased to meet you."

"Ciao Andriy."

"Ciao Kristen."

Ricky, who was still close by, had understood what was going on. He quickened his pace, leaving me behind. It struck me as strange behaviour.

"Ricky, where are you going?"

"I'm going back to listen to Russell Crowe. The concert is about to finish."

"Come on Ricky, come here a second. Did you see her?"

"Yes, Andriy…"

"Do you know her?"

"Yes, Andriy…"

"Ricky, you need to introduce me. She is marvellous."

"Andriy, let it go."

"What are you talking about, man? Have you gone mad?"

"Andriy, seriously, let it go."

"Why do you say that?"

"Kristen is the ex-girlfriend of Piersilvio Berlusconi."

The volume of the music was making me miss words.

"Of Silvio Berlusconi?"

"No, Andriy. Piersilvio, his son."

"Ah…"

"I know Kristen. I know Piersilvio. Don't make things

difficult for me, please."

"Listen, Ricky. Did you say ex-girlfriend?"

"Yes, they've not been together for a while."

"Well then, I'm not doing anything wrong, am I?"

"No, Andriy."

"Well then, I want to meet her properly. Please, Ricky."

"If that's the way things are, OK."

We invited her to our table. She was American. She didn't speak Italian well, and my English wasn't great, but we understood each other straight away. Everyone got hungry so we went for dinner at the Vecchio Porco restaurant. There were loads of us.

I was there with my group of friends, which included Sebastiano Rossi, our goalkeeper. She was there with her own group. We chatted away in a language that was purely ours: a strange jumble of words and feelings. At the end of the dinner, we swapped mobile numbers.

Over the following days, I stared at that number 100 times and, just before dialling it, I always changed my mind. I've always been shy and sensitive, something which has resulted in people sticking a thousand different labels on my back.

After two weeks, I had worked up the courage to make the call. I invited her to dinner at a small Japanese restaurant behind Parco Sempione – it was a nice little intimate place. We spoke with great honesty then went for a long drive, travelling as far as Como. I liked driving and listening to music. But above all else, I liked her. I took her home and, outside her front door, I kissed her for the first time.

We went out together again, and then again. We began to see each other frequently and to have a relationship. In the meantime, my sister had arrived in Milan from Ukraine, and so the Via Marina apartment was becoming a little crowded. Even though it was big, there was no guarantee of the privacy that Kristen and I were beginning to need. She was living with a friend.

Costacurta came to our rescue. He had just bought a new house and he let us have his old one, which was in Via Borgospesso, just off Via della Spiga, right in the middle of town. He sped up the removal timetable and moved into his new place while the crew were still finishing their work.

I had a lovely relaxing time with Kristen on the Costa Azzurra at the end of season 2000/1, even if I was still experiencing a little bit of irritability on account of my discussion with Galliani just before I left. In the middle of the holiday, I took a call from Leo Dell'Orco.

"Andriy, would you like to model for Giorgio Armani?"

"Me? On the catwalk?"

"Yes. On June 29, we'll present in Milan our spring-summer 2002 collection."

As she was a proper model, I spoke to Kristen about it.

"Andriy, why not?"

"Ok then, Leo. Thanks."

I called Galliani, because I needed Milan's permission to accept the offer. "No problem, Andriy. Go model for Armani, before you come back to model for us again. When you return, come see me in my office so we can sort out that little issue we left hanging."

Kristen was right; it was a lot of fun. Brad Pitt, Jennifer Aniston and George Clooney were all sitting in the front row. I had been warned to expect them, but I couldn't see anything. When I emerged from backstage to close that brilliant Armani show, the lights were so strong they almost blinded me. I felt my way along the catwalk with my feet. It didn't help that a thousand photographers' flashbulbs were going off at the same time.

Andriy, I'm begging you. Don't fall. Not here, not now. What an arse you would look.

Everything went well. The Hollywood actors even came to pay me compliments. Armani was happy, but he certainly didn't need my help to make his collections successful. I wasn't doing him a favour; it was him giving me a great gift.

Galliani called me. "Well done, my little model. I'll be waiting for you tomorrow morning."

I turned up punctually for the appointment, expecting to have to talk it through as we had the previous time. Not a bit of it.

"Andriy, it's all sorted."

"All sorted?"

"Yes, when you said no to Real Madrid, the president explained to you that we don't sell players. I'd expand that to say we don't sell players and they need to be happy. You'll have the salary you asked for."

I wasn't greedy. I never have been. I just knew I was worth what I was asking for. I've never had an agent for the sporting side of things; I've always preferred to deal directly with clubs about my future, without any intermediaries. At most, I've leaned on the experience of a couple of consultants, such as Oscar Damiani when I was at Milan. Leandro Cantamessa, the long-serving Milan club lawyer, assisted me with legal and bureaucratic matters.

Commercial deals are a different matter. On that side, Boris Becker was my first agent. Known as Boom Boom, he's a great guy, a former tennis world No.1 having won three Wimbledon titles, two Australian Opens and a US Open. He later opened an agency that represented athletes from many different disciplines.

My association with Becker immediately resulted in several sponsors. I signed up with Lotto, but when Boris asked me if he could be my agent for sporting matters too, I said no. It was thanks to him that I met Edoardo Artaldi, who became my friend and subsequently Novak Djokovic's manager.

I used to see Becker every now and then in Monte Carlo, but I never played tennis against him. It would have been another guaranteed massacre on the courts of the Country Club, and I just couldn't have put up with it.

My difference of opinion with Galliani having been smoothed over, the Milan team for season 2001/2 was taking shape. Pippo Inzaghi and Andrea Pirlo both arrived, along with a new coach, the Turk Fatih Terim, who was known as the Emperor.

One night, in the thick of the summer transfer market, Galliani invited Braida, me and a few of my teammates out to dinner. "Lads, there is an urgent issue to discuss. Rui Costa wants to come to Milan. He had a great time at Fiorentina under Terim, but Silvio Berlusconi has just become prime minister again and thinks it will make him unpopular to spend £35m on a single player. We need to convince him. If we don't sign Rui Costa, in a few hours he'll go to Lazio."

As we ate, Galliani's phone rang and his expression changed. He left his food, stood up and moved away. He reappeared a few minutes later, nodding over to me.

"Andriy, come with me a minute, please."

We went out of the restaurant. He handed me his phone and whispered, "it's President Berlusconi".

My expression changed as suddenly as his had earlier on.

"Ciao, Andriy."

"Good evening, Mr President."

"Andriy, what do you reckon about this Rui Costa?"

"Mr President, we need to sign him."

"I thought that might be your answer. Pass me back over to Galliani."

I took a few paces but still managed to eavesdrop.

"Yes, yes, Mr President. No problem, Mr President. Sure thing, Mr President. Thank you, Mr President."

When the call was finished, Galliani came over, looking as happy as he did in the middle of one of those trademark celebrations up in the stand. He gave me a big hug. Milan had just bought Rui Costa.

WHAT IF DAD DIES?

M<small>Y DISCUSSIONS</small> with Galliani, the product of having said no to Real Madrid.

The Costa Azzurra.

Modelling for Giorgio Armani.

Berlusconi and Rui Costa.

My niece Anastasia being born in Milan on August 8.

All things considered, summer 2001 was pretty intense. But more than anything, that summer belonged to my dad: on August 17, in the San Matteo hospital in Pavia, he underwent a heart transplant.

The situation had begun to deteriorate quickly several months before, during a routine test. Professor Vigano had taken me aside and said, "Andriy, unfortunately the bypasses are not helping your father as they should".

"So what can we do?"

"There is only one solution: a transplant."

They put his name on a database to try to find a suitable donor. I knew that the wait would be long and exhausting. I told mum the news, but we made a joint decision not to tell dad. Had he known about the procedure that was now necessary, he would have almost certainly withheld his consent. That was just his nature. And so we made the decision for him. Between probable life and certain death. There could be no other option than to try to keep him by our side.

He was ill. He could hardly walk and his heart was getting ever more enlarged. One lung wasn't working as it should have and so his breathing was always laboured. I spoke with mum in these dramatic moments and said: "We must do everything we can to ensure he makes it to the day of the operation."

Lobanovsky called me often from Ukraine to find out how he was doing. One time, I risked blowing our cover. I was explaining the situation to the Colonel and hadn't noticed dad walking right behind me. At the end of the call, mum came up to me all out of breath. "Your father heard you."

Dad asked me a question. "Were you speaking about a transplant?"

"Absolutely not; you picked me up wrong."

I don't know how, but he believed me. In order to feel better, he probably needed to deny to himself a truth that by now was blindingly obvious.

At the start of the summer, he insisted on going back to Kyiv. He loved spending the warmer months at home. I discussed it with Vigano, and he said that at that precise moment in time, there were no medical barrier to my father going on a flight.

And so my parents departed. Dad was happy and things

seemed to be on a positive path, in the sense that at least they were not getting worse. He got to rest up in the places that he held most dear while mum kept an eye on him to ensure he didn't do anything that was forbidden on account of it being dangerous to his health

I managed to carve out a few days for a trip to Bermuda with Kristen. On the way out, we were due to make a stop-off in New York before making our way to our final destination. When we reached the United States, however, I received a terrible phone call from mum.

"Andriy, dad doesn't feel well. I reckon he has pneumonia. But you know what he's like – he's refusing to go to the doctor. I'm trying to make him go. I'll keep you posted."

Later on, my phone rang again. A much lower tone of voice came through from late-night Kyiv.

"Ciao Andriy, how's it going?"

It was dad.

"I'm fine, and you?"

"I'm in hospital."

Mum had found him flat out on the ground and had called an ambulance.

"I'm in New York, dad, but tomorrow I'll be with you."

"I'll be waiting."

Kristen and I got on the first plane to Washington. She went to stay with her family in nearby Bethesda while I boarded a flight to Frankfurt. From there, I headed on to Ukraine. That phrase he had used – "I'll be waiting" – hammered away at me the whole way over. What if he was no longer there when I landed?

When I got to Frankfurt, I called home. He was still fighting. As soon as I landed in Kyiv, I dashed to the hospital. Dad was there and had kept his word – he had waited for me. In fact, he actually seemed better, or at least that's what he said. One of the doctors took me aside and told me a rather different truth: "Your father will not make it."

"In what sense, sorry?"

"His heart no longer works. He has two days left."

"That's not true."

"Mr Shevchenko…"

I closed my eyes, but reopened them immediately, not wanting to give up like this. I couldn't do that. I owed him as much, the man who had taught me never to give in. And so I called Vigano.

"Andriy, as soon as he's fit to fly, bring him to Pavia."

I called Rezo and alerted Milan. That night was hard. I hoped he wouldn't die. The 48 hours of which the Ukrainian doctor had spoken came and went; the countdown clock had proved incorrect. I spoke with Vigano again. He was worried about me.

"Andriy, can I give you some advice?"

"You can do whatever you want, professor."

"Good. Well, I'm advising you to come back to Milan. You need to rest. I know that training is about to start again."

"That's not up for discussion. I'll be here as long as I'm needed."

"Andriy, listen to me. There's no need for you to be there. Come back here and get yourself calm. I've taken a detailed look at your father's test results. Milan have already arranged for him to be transferred from Kyiv to Italy by air ambulance."

Berlusconi had taken care of everything. A memory flashed through my mind. That woman who worked for him at the villa in Sardinia. I put my trust in Vigano.

Back at Milanello for the first sessions of season

2001/2, it was impossible to focus purely on football. *What if dad dies?*

That accursed question would not let me be. I couldn't find a definitive response, but at the same time I could no longer live on hope alone. When I was advised that my father was finally ready to be transported to Italy, I asked Vigano: "Professor, will dad die?"

"Trust me, he won't die. In a few hours, he will be here with us, and me and my team will take care of him."

That's exactly what they did. His condition stabilised and at a certain point they discharged him from hospital to go home – his Milanese one. Now it was just a waiting game.

One fine day, Vigano called us up: "Come, come. It's time."

On August 17, 2001, dad got a new heart. Thanks to whom, I'll never know, and that's only right and proper. Because one life saved always corresponds to one that has just been lost. The heart of a person no longer here is immediately transplanted into someone else in the hope that it will save them.

The donor gives infinite joy to the family of the recipient, but for their own family, all that's left is the immense pain of loss. Had I known the identity of the person who allowed my dad to live, how could I have ever approached their relatives to say thanks? With what words and gestures could I have convinced them that, in some way, they should be happy too?

The only certainty is that when they were alive, that nameless person took a massive decision. A decision that, following their example, I have made my own: my organs will be donated.

The surgery was a complete success. For two weeks, Berlusconi phoned me continually to find out about my father's post-operative progress. So did Galliani and Braida. Rezo was my shadow. Without their substantial help, the happy ending would never have been written.

Terim and my teammates kept telling me that I could count on them for anything, while from Ukraine, Lobanovsky and the Surkis brothers requested daily updates. Each afternoon, at the end of training, I went to Pavia to visit dad.

One night, I invited Vigano to dinner. He talked to me about his job, detailing the satisfactions and the anguish. I asked him a rather odd question: "Professor, can I come to watch a transplant operation?"

"Would you not be scared, Andriy?"

"No."

I am a curious person, and it would also allow me to understand what dad had gone through. I wanted to know every detail, to put a face to the name of that enemy whom our whole family had fought. Besides, I'm never struck by panic. Whenever I'm in an unusually complicated situation, I just up my concentration. Another of Lobanovsky's lessons. My brain starts to work better, looking for solutions. Nonetheless, Vigano gave a little laugh. He probably thought I wasn't being serious.

Two weeks later, at around 11pm, I received a call.

"Andriy…"

"What's happened to my father?"

"Nothing, he's fine. But are you ready?"

"For what?"

"To come here. I'm about to go into the operating theatre."

Around 1am, I arrived at the San Matteo hospital where Vigano was waiting for me.

"Hurry up, Andriy, the patient is ready and the new heart

is on its way." They disinfected me, cleaned me, dressed me. When Vigano gave me the nod, I went into the theatre. As he carried out the procedure, he explained every detail of what was happening, step after step, cut after cut.

I stayed calm the whole time. I saw an open chest and various organs. The patient was a smoker, and the prof showed me some small black marks stuck to his lungs: nicotine residue.

As he transplanted the heart, he spoke to me about the effect of the various drugs that had been administered to my father and then prescribed for his rehabilitation. I was struck by the absolute certainty that Vigano, and those like him, are true geniuses.

If I missed a shot, people whistled.

If they made a mistake, people died.

ANCELOTTI SITS DOWN,
PIRLO STANDS UP

Terim was a different kind of coach to the ones I had worked with before. He gave the players a lot of freedom, especially when it came to rules. He brought a whole new philosophy to Milanello and the training sessions were not as tough as those of his predecessors.

I got on with him – our relationship was direct and to the point. He certainly did not have luck on his side, with Rui Costa, a player he had been desperate to sign, breaking his hand in two places in the very first match of the league season against Brescia.

The Emperor lasted only 10 Serie A games, which was still time enough for him to enjoy a derby win over Inter. We came from behind to win 4-2, with me scoring a double. Berlusconi decided to sack him in November 2001, after a 1-0 away defeat by Torino, in which Cristiano scored. Cristiano Lucarelli. I was upset, because any sacking represents a collective failure. In the meantime, I was desperately missing Kristen, who had been forced to stay in the United States after the September 11 attacks. We spoke loads on the phone, but the world was changing rapidly and I realised there was a big part of mine missing. A piece of me was in another continent on the other side of the ocean, imprisoned by unknown forces and perhaps under attack. As the days went by, I felt more and more nostalgic about the time we had spent together.

"Kristen, when are you coming back?"

I asked her that question continually, but in reality it wasn't up to her. The air space was still closed. I was really worried: she is American and Americans had become a target. The Twin Towers, The Pentagon, United Airlines Flight 93: death had fallen out of the sky. I was scared that something bad might happen to her.

As soon as it was allowed – as soon as the pandemic of suspicion towards other people diminished to more acceptable levels – Kristen returned to Milan and we sat down to talk.

"Andriy, after everything that's happened, I'm thinking about moving back to America permanently."

"America?"

"My rental agreement is about to expire and in a few days my mother will arrive to help me with the move."

"Kristen, listen, stay here with me. We've got the apartment that Billy Costacurta gave us – let's try to live together and see how it works out."

"But Andriy…"

"Kristen, listen, I can't be without you anymore. You're everything to me, my most beautiful thought. It killed me when you weren't here. I, I…"

"You?"

"I love you, Kristen."

Her eyes misted over and mine too. We got emotional together, crying happy tears in silence. And then we resumed speaking; more free and even more happy.

"Andriy, we've been together for a while and you've never said these things to me before. Why?"

"Because, when I had you here with me, I perhaps took certain feelings for granted. But from the moment I couldn't actually see you, I was struggling to breathe. Stay with me, please."

"Andriy…"

"Kristen…"

"OK."

"What did you say, Kristen?

"I said yes, Andriy. This is what I want. Let's stay together in Milan."

I loved her. Loved her with all my being. I would have followed her to Bethesda had it been necessary. Sure enough, her mum did come to Milan to give her a hand with the move, but only in the direction of the apartment on Via Borgospesso. Our refuge.

Sparks were about to fly on the pitch as well – with Carlo Ancelotti, who had replaced Fatih Terim. As a Milan midfielder, he had won the lot: two *scudetti*, an Italian Supercup, two European Cups, two European Supercups and an Intercontinental Cup. A real master of the sport in Italy, Europe and the wider world, just as Berlusconi required.

Now he was about to try again as coach. Lots of guys in the dressing room already knew him, starting with Maldini and Costacurta. For his presentation at Milanello, the president arrived by helicopter; always a good sign.

First impressions were excellent. At training, he spoke

to you as a coach, a boss, and nothing more, but elsewhere he was one of us. A player among players. No topic of conversation was forbidden, he would tell jokes and muck around, and if you had a problem, you knew that he would listen. That he would help you solve it.

It was easy for us to tell when he was happy: he would be eating more than normal. He immediately clocked Pirlo, who had not played much under Terim. As teammates, we had known for a long time just how good he was – every time he took to the training field, he turned it into a show for us. The best technical player I've ever seen – he treated the ball with respect.

When he was under pressure, he kept it. When all hell was breaking loose around him, he kept it. When they were marking him tightly, perhaps even doubling up, he kept it. And then suddenly, he would be picking out the striker high up the pitch, with impeccable timing and reading his movements perfectly. He could thread the ball through the tiniest spaces: he saw tunnels where everyone else saw nothing. He danced to his own tune, on his own individual stage.

We used to speak about it in the dressing room when he wasn't around to hear.

"Why does this guy never play?"

As soon as Carlo arrived on the bench, there was no longer any need to ask. The moment he sat down, Andrea stood up. Carlo played him in front of the defence, giving him even more space and time to do his thing.

The one thing about Pirlo that never changed was his expression, which stayed exactly the same 24 hours a day. It was impossible to tell whether he was happy or angry and he took advantage of this, especially with Gattuso, who was his preferred victim for jokes. He would tell him crazy, invented things which Rino took to be the truth. He'd then tell him the truth, which Rino took as an invention. Andrea drove him mad, but they forged a tight bond from day one.

I remember a fight breaking out on the training pitch between two teammates. Ancelotti sent everyone back to the dressing room, and the last to enter was Andrea who appeared with two boxing gloves that he had taken from the Milanello gym. He gave one to each contender, and the pair of them burst out laughing. No more tension, problem solved.

Andrea had personality and the group as a whole was growing. A great Milan team was starting to emerge. You could feel the energy building even as we suffered a whole load of injuries that season, notably Pippo Inzaghi's.

And mine.

When I was fit, I scored goals. By December 2001, I was already on 14; 11 in the league and three in the UEFA Cup. At the start of 2002, the numbers diminished drastically.

One afternoon, during a small-sided training match at Milanello, I was about to receive the ball. Martin Laursen tackled me hard from behind. Our teammates told him off. "It would be better if you actually made those kind of challenges in a game as well."

In the following days, I continued to train. It seemed like it was just a big bruise and nothing more, but I was in real pain. I couldn't run, never mind kick. But I wanted to keep moving, so I tried a little bit of light running and spent time in the gym. Every little movement was accompanied by a burst of pain.

I've always been bad at staying still, right back to my Dynamo Kyiv days. This one time, Lobanovsky had dismissed a doctor who advised me to miss a training session because I had a 39°C fever. The Colonel burst into my room and ordered me to get on the pitch straight away, because my teammates were there waiting.

And so, here at Milan it took a bit of time before I convinced myself that it wasn't the right moment to push. In the meantime, I had kept on working. But I just wasn't getting better.

Thanks to Rudy Tavana, the club doctor with whom I've always had a great relationship, and a few specific tests, I discovered that I had suffered a muscle tear. Laursen's kick had struck an area where I had a scar from an old injury. As the tissue there wasn't very elastic, it had torn. Where normally the blow can be absorbed, in this state the muscle tore. The medical staff ordered me to stop training.

That was the case right up until April 4, 2002, when the first leg of our UEFA Cup semi-final brought strictly one-way traffic. We lost 4-0 away from home to Borussia Dortmund with Amoroso scoring a hat-trick and Heinrich supplying the other. The Westfalenstadion was a living hell that night. The second leg was scheduled for the following week at San Siro.

Galliani began to insist. "Andriy, we need you. You have to play."

Ancelotti was on the same wavelength. "Sheva, grit your teeth, we need to attempt a comeback."

I didn't hold back – I would never do that – but the fact remained that I had not properly healed and I ended up playing poorly. We were 3-0 up after 93 minutes, only for Ricken to score and send the Germans through 5-3 on aggregate.

I was sent out to play in the league as well. I started to receive criticism from abroad, with some journalists writing that I wanted to leave Milan and was distracted by other thoughts.

Galliani was worried and asked me to meet him. "Andriy, is something wrong?"

"Mr Galliani, making me play so soon was a mistake. I didn't feel right. Many times in my career it's been me forcing things, for the good of the team, but I'm convinced that when it comes to serious injuries, it's better to recover completely before throwing yourself back in the mix. That's not what happened here."

It was a complicated end to the season for me. I was no longer myself and my best form was a distant memory. The last two games were decisive for our league campaign. We won 2-1 away to Verona then beat Lecce 3-0 at San Siro, with me scoring one of the goals. Right at the death, we had managed to claim fourth place, behind Juventus, Roma and Inter but one point clear of Chievo, the big surprise package, and two clear of Lazio.

We would be back in the Champions League the following year – the legendary season 2002/3.

EUROPE LOOKS
FOR ITS QUEEN

ALESSANDRO NESTA. Clarence Seedorf. Rivaldo. Golf. These were the four summer signings that stood out. The first three made by Milan, and the last one by me.

It's a sporting discipline that I'd discovered a few months previously, thanks to a friend of mine, Manuel, who lived in the countryside next to a driving range.

He asked me if I wanted to give it a go and I said yes, out of curiosity and politeness more than anything else. Instinctively, I played right-handed and it didn't go well. I then tried with my left, and the ball began to travel. It's funny, my left was the stronger one when it came to ice hockey too, even though I'm naturally right-handed.

I thought it was going to be a one-time thing, but during our end-of-season holiday to Bermuda, golf got me good and proper. On the first day, I enjoyed the beach. The second day as well. But on the third, I began to get bored.

Kristen suggested that I go and play a round at the golf course near to where we were staying.

"It's not the game for me. I tried and I'm not very good."

"Try again, Andriy."

She knew me. And she knew golf, having grown up at the Bethesda Congressional, a real reference point for lovers of the sport. She had been an excellent swimmer, training to become part of the US national teams, but every now and then she had spent some time on the green.

There had come a point where she had to choose between the swimming pool and the catwalk and she opted to become a full-time model. Her father, Mike, had been a pitcher for the Minnesota Twins in MLB.

And she was right. Golf began to hook me. Because of the way I'm made, whenever I messed up a shot, I felt the need to come back as soon as I possibly could so that I never messed it up again. So, I got better.

Every morning of that holiday, I'd hire out the equipment and play. In the afternoon, I would swim, and in the evening I would run. I was in pretty decent shape by the time I turned up at Milanello for the start of season 2002/3.

By August 14, we were already playing a competitive match, against Slovan Liberec at San Siro in the first leg of a Champions League qualifier. We won 1-0, thanks to a goal from Inzaghi.

Ten minutes from the end, I felt a strange movement. My knee had started acting up and it was hurting. In such cases, the diagnosis is never immediate – you have to wait and hope.

Ancelotti gave us two days off and I jumped in the car with Kristen to head to Monte Carlo. I did the driving. It was almost night when we arrived, and I went straight to bed. The next morning, my knee looked really swollen and

My Life, My Football

the pain was worse. I called Tavana. "Doctor, something is not right here."

"In Monte Carlo?"

"No, in my knee."

"I'll take a look tomorrow."

And so, we got back in the car and set off for Milan, with me driving again. The outcome of Tavana's assessment and the subsequent tests was a real cold shower: I had suffered a lateral meniscus tear. I have always had a high pain threshold and so find it hard to tell when I have hurt myself badly. That's what had happened here.

"Andriy, I'm sorry. You need an operation."

I flew to Antwerp in Belgium to see Professor Marc Mertens, who carried out the surgery. I then came back to Milanello for my rehabilitation. Next stop? Antwerp again, for a check-up and some physio.

I was working on it twice a day, every day. In Belgium, when it got dark, it was almost as if a curfew was in place. People ate early and the city – a lovely spot – became deserted. In the middle of town there was only silence. I walked around, lost in thought. I loved the views: colours and imagination – mine. I was imagining matches.

First I walked and then I ran. When I began to increase the load to strengthen the muscle, I took it too far and the knee swelled up again. Tavana – a man who never got annoyed – did so on this occasion.

"Andriy, now you really need to take it easy."

On August 28, I put a scarf around my neck and became a fan. *Forza Milan*. We were playing the second leg of the Slovan Liberec tie away from home. We lost 2-1 but still qualified. We were back at the top table of the Champions League.

In the meantime, Ancelotti had mapped out a Milan

team with Inzaghi as a reference point. He was the only striker in a 4-3-2-1; the so-called Christmas tree formation. At that point in time, it was a celebration for other people. I was still an unopened gift.

The team were going well and scoring lots of goals. In Serie A, they notched three against Modena on September 14 (Inzaghi scoring twice), three against Perugia on September 21 (Inzaghi scoring once), one against Lazio the following week, six against Torino on October 6 (Inzaghi scoring a hat-trick) and four against Atalanta a fortnight later.

In the Champions League, they scored two against Lens on September 18 (Inzaghi double), four against Deportivo La Coruna on September 24 (Inzaghi hat-trick), and two against Bayern Munich on October 1 (Inzaghi double). On October 24, they put another two past the Germans, with Inzaghi scoring once.

While all this was going on, I had resumed full training and felt ready. I was fit but wasn't playing. I was left to watch. At the end of one training session at Milanello, I knocked on the coach's door.

"Carlo, can I speak to you?"

"Yes, obviously, Andriy."

"Listen, Carlo. I understand. I was injured, you changed the formation and there's only one striker. I just need to tell you that I'm not happy. I'm getting stronger, I feel good and I want to play more."

"Look, Andriy, I want to be clear with you as well. We're playing this way now and we're winning, so I have no intention of changing. We'll keep doing what we're doing – Pippo is scoring every week. You just need to wait for your chance."

If we were playing at San Siro and I didn't start, at

full-time I would jump in the car and head to Milanello with Rezo. I'd train on my own, running and shooting, doing exercises. The following day, I would come back for normal training with the others. I couldn't stay still: as Lobanovsky used to say, my body would have reacted badly. I would have lost my rhythm. Ninety minutes made all the difference in the world.

After my chat with Ancelotti, I asked for a meeting with Galliani.

"Andriy, why the long face?"

"Mr Galliani, I never play. I think it's time for me to try somewhere else, especially if things carry on like this."

"Andriy, this is your home. Don't even think about leaving. Let's see how things go and then we'll speak again in December."

It was October. I was convinced I would leave Milan. I also spoke to Oscar Darmian, asking him to have a look around and find out where I could go. There is always a big club looking for a striker.

I got a few minutes here and there, little crumbs of action. Often, I was left among the reserves. And then, on November 26, 2002, in the first round of fixtures in the second group phase of the Champions League, my big opportunity arrived.

More specifically, Real Madrid arrived at San Siro. A side with men like Roberto Carlos, Figo, Zidane, Raul, Morientes. Because they were playing all the time, a few of my teammates were tired. Inzaghi was one of them. Ancelotti gave me a call.

"Pippo needs a rest. Andriy, it's your turn."

"Carlo, I'm ready."

I considered it one of my last chances. Perhaps the very last. I needed to play well and score. I played well and scored. I felt strength in my legs, and my mind was free. I got in behind to put us ahead after 40 minutes. I owed a big thanks to Rui Costa for the assist. One Manuel had helped me discover golf; another Manuel allowed me to rediscover Milan.

I was back thinking clearly again, something I had missed. The 4-3-2-1 became a 4-3-1-2 with both me and Inzaghi up front. The two of us together in the belief that something unique might happen. A new calendar – it was Christmas for me too.

We were top of Serie A at the halfway stage but wouldn't go on to win the title. The Champions League was occupying our thoughts. Europe was looking for its queen. After that Madrid game at San Siro, we kept on the right path, despite a few incidents on the way.

Borussia Dortmund 0-1 Milan
Milan 1-0 Lokomotiv Moscow
Lokomotiv Moscow 0-1 Milan
Real Madrid 3-1 Milan
Milan 0-1 Borussia Dortmund

The final group table showed Milan on 12 points, Real Madrid with 11, Dortmund with 10 and Lokomotiv Moscow, one. It was us and the Spaniards through to the quarter-finals, where we would meet Zlatan Ibrahimovic's Ajax. Young, tough opponents. It finished 0-0 in Amsterdam, with the return leg proving altogether livelier.

1-0 to us after 30 minutes, Inzaghi
1-1 after 63 minutes, Litmanen
2-1 to us after 65 minutes, me
2-2 after 78 minutes, Pienaar

In the 90th minute it was still 2-2. Ajax were about to go through on away goals while we – who still didn't feel lost, even in that moment – were one step away from destroying our season.

However.

In the 91st minute, an immense Brocchi (who had moved to full-back), managed to get away from the pressing of Ibrahimovic – who wanted to bite his ankle – right beside one of the corner flags at our end. Brocchi gave me the ball.

I saw that Nesta was free on the far side of the box, and so I passed to him.

Nesta gave the ball to Costacurta, who began to run forwards.

Maldini pulled out a perfect through ball for Ambrosini, who was right on the edge of the Ajax penalty area.

Ambrosini, in a flash, headed the ball to Inzaghi, who was stationed in the box (Inzaghi was always stationed in the box).

Inzaghi produced a little dink that took out Lobont, the Ajax goalkeeper.

Tomasson, doing his best Inzaghi impression, to remove any doubt did not wait for the ball to go over the line. From a millimetre out, he touched it, and knocked it into the back of the net. Pinching the goal and gifting us a 3-2 win that threw open the doors to the next round.

In the semi-finals, we were going to play Inter.

THANK YOU,
VALERIJ VASILEVIC

MAY 7, 2003, San Siro: Milan 0-0 Inter. Our team for the first leg: Dida, Costacurta, Nesta, Maldini, Kaladze, Gattuso, Brocchi, Seedorf, Rui Costa, Me, Inzaghi... Serpelloni Piero

May 13, 2003, San Siro: Inter 1-1 Milan. Our team for the second leg: Abbiati, Costacurta, Nesta, Maldini, Kaladze, Gattuso, Pirlo, Seedorf, Rui Costa, Me, Inzaghi... Serpelloni Piero.

There's no way we weren't going through: we had 12 men both times.

Every now and then, right out of the blue – almost as if it was a timeless entity, a prank played by the past – I felt the blow that Laursen had given me in training. This sudden pain returned a few days before the first European derby. I didn't know what to do, and so I discussed it with my teammates.

In the dressing room at Milanello, Pirlo came up to me.
"Andriy, can I give you some advice?"

He had his usual expression, so I didn't know whether he was about to play a trick or genuinely wanted to help me. The second option was the better of the two. This was such an important moment – for him as well as me. For the whole of Milan, in fact. This was our moment.

"Certainly, Andrea."

"I know someone in Brescia…"

A trusted physiotherapist whom he had always used. He gave me the number, I arranged an appointment and headed there to meet him. In front of me was a giant of a man, who must have weighed around 16 stones.

"Pleased to meet you. I'm Piero. Serpelloni Piero."

First his name, then his surname, then his first name again. Imagine if in the 007 films, the secret agent with license to kill introduced himself like this: "I'm James. Bond James." It would sound sincere yet distinctly strange.

What's certain is that Serpelloni Piero, or Piero Serpelloni, was quite brilliant. He gave me a two-hour massage, basically breaking me. That night, I was in pieces, the following morning a footballer reborn. Ready to take on Inter. Ready for anything.

From that moment on, I've never left him and many of my successes have borne his imprint too. A rather big imprint, it must be said, considering the force that he used. I loved the Milanello physios and I loved him: together, they were the Dream Team of muscles.

The day of that first game against Inter I felt really good, serene. Wake up, training, shower, lunch, golf on the PlayStation, two-hour nap, a little bit of music, slice of cake and fresh fruit juice, team meeting, last few bits and pieces into my trolley case, onto the bus to San Siro.

My Life, My Football

It was my usual routine, but my heart was beating differently. I could hear it shouting in my chest, battering away. It was reclaiming its space and sending me a clear message: you can't survive on tactics alone. Organisation and romanticism, that's the formula to note down and discover.

On the pitch, it was a chess match. A psychological battle that finished 0-0 which for us looked a decent result, given that we had technically been playing at home. In the return leg, each of our goals would count double. We had kept the back door shut and guaranteed ourselves another week of relative calm, or as close to it as you can manage in circumstances like that.

Between one derby and the next, on May 10 we lost to Brescia in the league, but it didn't matter. We were upset, of course, but that's all there was to it. And then it was all about Inter again. All about San Siro and that well-rehearsed timetable, that list of things to do while the shivers went down your spine.

We went ahead with a goal from me in the first minute of first-half stoppage time. Seedorf supplied the assist, I tried to dribble Cordoba and there was a little coming together between my left foot and his right leg. I struck the ball on the slide and lifted it over Toldo. I had scored falling over. A sweet, sweet fall.

Our opponents equalised in the 83rd minute thanks to Obafemi Martins, who celebrated with three backflips and a somersault. Right before the end, Abbiati saved a Kallon shot with his calf. And that's how it ended. 1-1, to us, because that draw had the taste of victory.

I lost my head with joy: we were in the final of the Champions League. I ran around, laughing and shouting. And then, far from prying eyes, I stopped and lifted my gaze. Looking at the stars I said thank you. *Thank you, Valerij Vasilevic.*

Exactly one year before, on May 13, 2002, Lobanovsky had passed away. Moved to another sky. I was in New York with Milan for a tournament but wasn't actually playing as I recovered from a nose operation. The terrible news arrived from Kyiv. At 63 years old, the Colonel had felt unwell during a Dynamo away game against Metalurh Zaporizzja, and had never recovered.

It was hard. It was as if, in that precise moment, my world had lost a bit of light, a bit of hope, a bit of safety. It was intimately devastating. I left the United States for Ukraine, exactly as I had when hoping to find my dad still alive. They set up a temporary funeral home in the Dynamo stadium and the whole city turned out to pay its respects. On the day of the funeral itself, there were close to 200,000 people on the streets. A human tide, a tsunami of pure love. Some were giving the last salute to a hero, others to a father of the nation, me to the man who had changed my life, and not just my sporting one.

I was thinking irrational thoughts. I hoped that he would wake from that eternal sleep, sending away the doctor who had misdiagnosed him, there in front of everyone, just as he had that medic who tried to have me miss training because of a fever.

In Ukraine, it is traditional to arrange a big meal after the funeral to honour the deceased. One last gathering before the final journey. We former Dynamo players arranged to meet in a restaurant, and there we remembered him. With tears and alcohol.

On that magical night at San Siro, I dedicated us reaching the final to him. But it wasn't enough – I owed him more. A year had gone by, but it seemed like only yesterday.

A truly painful wound, a billion times worse than the one that Laursen had given me.

Winning the Champions League became an obsession for me, even more than it already was. I made a silent promise to him: *I'll win it and bring it to you.* For the first time in my life, I used the familiar form of address. Perhaps because I thought it might help reduce the distance. Not between us, but between the place where I was and the highest point up there where the final illness had sent him.

We didn't yet know who we were going to face, but we knew the venue. Manchester United's Old Trafford, The Theatre of Dreams.

The second leg of the other semi-final, between Juventus and Real Madrid, was due to be played the night after ours. In the first game, at the Santiago Bernabeu, the Spaniards had won 2-1. Back home, Lippi's team defied all expectations to win 3-1 and set up another all-Italian head-to-head.

Before that, there was another piece of business to take care of, and a not insignificant one at that: the first leg of the Coppa Italia final against Roma, scheduled for eight days before the Champions League showpiece. We took to the field at the Stadio Olimpico on May 20. We knew we couldn't take them or the occasion lightly. A trophy is always a trophy.

It went well. We won 4-1. Totti opened the scoring, but we equalised through Serginho before going ahead thanks to an Ambrosini goal. Serginho scored again, before I got the last one, having started on the bench.

We had gone well beyond the cliche chucked out by managers and players even on the first day of the season. For that Milan team, every game really was a cup final.

In the following days, I studied Ancelotti at Milanello.

His eyes were more alive than ever, and he could barely hide his desire to take revenge on an environment that hadn't appreciated him. On a fanbase who had chanted 'a pig can't coach'. They said he always finished second. He'd been right at home in Rome as a player. Decidedly less so in Turin as a manager. In the space of a week, he was encountering two of his old flames. One eternal, just like the city around it, and another which had ended badly, without ever being consummated.

We were working brilliantly as the clock ticked down. We seemed to be in a perfect place. Berlusconi came to see us in his helicopter. Galliani made ceaseless, frenetic trips between his office and the trophy room in the Via Turati base. He would stare at the five European Cups on the shelf and wonder where to put the sixth, as and when it arrived. He would shake his head and come back, making superstitious gestures. And then the whole cycle would start over again.

Braida was always playing with his hair.

Maldini was calm.

Costacurta was serene.

Both of them had already lifted the trophy three times and knew what was required. Seeing how they were gave us confidence and strength. The rest of us players really studied them, even though we knew them and their characters off by heart. We were looking for new details, unusual glances, little details to develop. They were two living, breathing instruction books: read these and everything will be less complicated.

We inundated them with questions and they had an answer for everything and everyone. Having reference points like them in the dressing room made the build-up easier, your sleep less tormented. They were the guiding lights for the journey we were about to undertake, and staring at them didn't hurt your eyes.

The whole of Milanello held us in its embrace. It really is a fairytale kingdom filled with fantastic people. Kings and queens who might not have had a throne, but did have our utmost admiration.

The employees at Milan's training centre began playing that final long before we did. They worked tirelessly to ensure we wanted for nothing. The cooks. The waiters. The cleaning staff. The security guards. Every one of them for every one of us: long live the red-and-black musketeers. They were on hand 24 hours a day for every need, every eventuality.

The famous room with the hearth was where the team tended to meet. It was a good place to chat, to talk about what was about to happen. To laugh and joke after training.

Every now and then I would arrive in there a little late, straight from the pitch.

"Where were you, Sheva?"

"Sorry lads, I was practising my penalties."

NO CARLO, I'LL TAKE
THE LAST ONE

Mottram Hall had an 18-hole golf course. Our pre-match hotel in England was a truly peaceful oasis. For the team, three days of external harmony and inner tumult in Macclesfield, just outside Manchester. Classical music just before a rock concert.

I had a room with a view. Namely, of the golf course. Throwing open the windows a few hours before the final, I noticed Inzaghi walking the greens. He was on his own, speaking to himself. He was mimicking movements and shots, dribbling opponents of whose presence only he was aware.

He'd turn around, face straight ahead again then sprint for a few metres. He would then check he hadn't ended up offside. He was playing Juventus, without Juventus being there. The waiting game was intense for him.

I closed the windows and went to sleep. Nap time was

allotted in our schedule for those who managed to fall asleep. I succeeded, driven on by my dreams.

I woke back up at Old Trafford. The dressing rooms were small and not very comfortable. A heavy silence hung over those four walls. I taped up my ankles and followed the dress code stated on the invitation. On went my No.7 shirt. It looked even more beautiful than normal. Shinier, somehow.

I went out onto the pitch for the warm-up. To get there, you went down a short, wide tunnel. From the shadows into the spotlight in the space of a few metres. From an insulated room to a resounding roar. What a sight it was. A stadium split in two, a little bit of us and a little bit of them; room for everyone, at least to begin with.

Kirsten was up in the stand with her family and mine, as well as my friends and ours. Nesta came over to me just before we started a ball drill.

"I'm struggling to breathe, Andriy."

"I'm the same, Sandro."

The emotion of the night was contagious.

We went back down the tunnel, exchanging a few words with Berlusconi and the directors before listening to Ancelotti's final instructions. It was showtime.

I was third in line, behind the captain, Maldini, and my good friend Kaladze. Next up was Gattuso, who was already covering my back. Growling away at the world.

And there she was outside the tunnel. The Champions League trophy. It's supposed to be bad luck to touch it before winning it, but I reckon only insecure people think like that. She was flashy, elegant, simply marvellous – the only thing in the world more beautiful was Kristen.

In that precise moment, I felt like I loved them both, and that made me feel guilty. I approached the trophy and gave it a quick touch. It was like an electric shock – energy flooding through me.

The game began.

"Sandro, are you feeling better?

"Not yet, Andriy. You?"

"Me neither."

Five minutes later, the tension had disappeared. Piece by piece, blow by blow. We moved forward a centimetre at a time. It wasn't the most aesthetically pleasing game of all time, but nobody gave an inch.

Near the start, I scored but it was disallowed. Buffon then saved an Inzaghi shot. When he came on for Juventus, Antonio Conte hit the bar.

0-0 after 90 minutes.

0-0 after 120 minutes, with Roque Junior still in the thick of the battle despite having suffered an injury.

And so, to penalties.

Ancelotti gathered us in a circle to read out the list of takers.

"Andriy, you'll go first or second."

"No Carlo, I'll take the last one."

Those who call it a lottery are mistaken. They believe it all comes down to luck, whereas it's the human factor that is decisive. On the eve of the match, I had been practicing penalties again.

Juventus went first.

Trezeguet: saved by Dida. 0-0
Serginho: Scored. 1-0 to Milan
Birinidelli: Scored. 1-1
Seedorf: saved by Buffon. Still 1-1
Zalayeta: saved by Dida. 1-1 to the bitter end.
Kaladze: saved by Buffon. Still 1-1

No Carlo, I'll take the last one   157

Montero: saved by Dida. 1-1, for the last time
Nesta: Scored. 2-1 to us
Del Piero: Scored. 2-2

Three Juventus misses, two for Milan. It was my turn. Nesta had something urgent to tell me: "If you score, we're champions of Europe." He had got his breath back.

From the centre circle to the penalty spot is like walking to the moon, even though it's only 40 metres. Shpakov, Chernobyl, Dad, Mum, my sister, my dead friends, that time in Agropoli, the needle with which I sewed the Ian Rush boots, the folks who had failed me in the university entrance exam. Yes, those guys. Lysenko, Onyshchenko, the Dynamo Reserves, the spectre of military school, Ukraine's independence, Sabo, Pavlov, Rebrov and his radio gear, Lobanovsky, Rezo, the national team shirt, Galbiati's scouting report, Camp Nou, the Surkis brothers, the Dynamo first team, the secret service security detail. Never mind Milan and all the people there.

It's incredible how many thoughts, how many people, can fit into so little space and so little time. Blasts from the past that you thought had been and gone. You're there all alone, repeating the same phrase over and over. *Andriy, whatever happens, once you've decided which side you're going, don't change your mind.*

I picked up the ball and put it on the spot. It was heavy. The referee was called Markus Merk, a German. I looked at him. Then I looked at Buffon. Then the referee again and back to Buffon. Four times over, until the referee gave me a nod. *You can take it, Shevchenko.*

The noise of the crowd had covered up the blast of his whistle. Had he not gestured to me, who knows how long I would have spent still staring into his eyes.

Stay calm, Andriy. Those were the last words I allowed myself.

I ran my tongue over my bottom lip. It was dry.

The run-up.

The strike.

Buffon moved to his right, I went to his left.

Goal.

3-2.

Milan, champions of Europe.

I gave my first embrace to Dida. You might think that I chose him because he had played a decisive role with the saves from Trezeguet, Zalayeta and Montero, but the reality is less poetic. He was simply the first guy I came across on my mad run with no destination in mind. I then went looking for a Ukrainian flag to carry on our lap of honour. I knew where I came from.

Paolo Maldini lifting the trophy is an unforgettable image that is tattooed on my brain. You can't see it, but it's there. A precious corner of my memory that will never disappear. When he passed the cup to me, I understood that this was really happening. It was all real.

So many photos, so many handshakes. Back in the dressing room, we met up with Berlusconi, Galliani and Braida. Toasts. Songs. When everyone was out, I didn't even have the strength to walk to the shower. The warning light was flashing: I was running on fumes.

I tied the towel around my waist, lay down in a corner and went to sleep for 20 minutes, utterly drained by the fatigue and nervous tension of the game. I then had a wash and we all went back to the hotel, where our family and friends were waiting. I gave one kiss to Kristen and one to the trophy – I still felt a bit confused. There was wine and dozens of crates of beer. After a few, Serginho was adamant that Ancelotti was his father.

At five in the morning, we invaded the golf course, using it like a football pitch and recreating the match from Old Trafford. It was Milan against Milan, so we were sure to win again. When we started out, there were 18 holes, and then came Gattuso, with all the delicacy of a plough. There were more than 18 by the time we finished off.

The miracle of Macclesfield: the multiplication of bogeys and eagles. Goals above and below par.

And a sixth European Cup on the mantelpiece. Galliani was gloating. He had been right to secretly take the measurements in the trophy room. As soon as we got back from Manchester, he would display her in a spot that he had already allocated. Right next to her five twins.

CAN I TAKE THE TROPHY
TO UKRAINE?

DURING our descent, you could see Milanello. On May 29, 2003, we fastened our seatbelts and landed at Malpensa Airport. One captain (of the plane) opened the window of the cockpit to fly a black-and-red flag. Another captain (of Milan) got ready with Ancelotti to show off the Champions League trophy at the top of the stairs.

Thousands of people were waiting for us, and their happiness was also ours. But Carlo had a mental Post-it note for us: "Lads, we still need to win the Coppa Italia. The final is in two days. By the way, Andriy, are you going to make it?"

"Boss, sadly this time I can't help you."

I wouldn't have lasted 30 seconds. Physically, I was in bits. I'd left everything in Manchester. San Siro was full to the rafters for the second leg against Roma. 76,000 fans wanted to applaud the new European champions, but our opponents had different ideas. Especially Francesco Totti, who scored twice in the second half to put his side 2-0 up. Even though we had won the first game 4-1, goals from Rivaldo then Inzaghi made us feel a little more relieved. The match finished 2-2. Pippo scored in the 94th minute, having been on the field from the first. We had won the Coppa Italia too.

A big party had been arranged in our honour at Milan's Sforzesco Castle, but I couldn't stay long. My season was not yet over – I still had national team games to play. Before departing, I had another frank, sincere conversation with Ancelotti.

"We beat Juventus at Old Trafford, and I know how much that meant to you. I'm extremely happy for you, for us, and obviously for me and my decisive penalty. I'll remind you that during the course of the season, when you left me out, it really upset me…"

I gave a little nod to the role played by Tassotti, his assistant. We had become friends immediately. "Mauro was very important for me. We spent a lot of time together at the end of team sessions, working on technique. In difficult moments, he had my back and explained to me why, tactically, it was impossible to start me in games."

I carried on my tour by visiting Galliani in his office. I had a particular request to make of him.

"Mr Galliani, can I take the Champions League trophy to Ukraine?"

His face lit up.

"Come, come with me Sheva. Follow me, quick."

He accompanied me to the trophy room straight from his desk. He was just about pulling me along by the hand. There was no longer any doubt: this was his favourite path in the world.

He pointed towards the most beautiful shelf.

"Andriy, choose the one you want. There are six of them."

I indicated the last one, the sixth, the newest one, the original. I took it on board a private flight to Kyiv. My home.

I took the trophy to Lobanovsky's statue, outside the Dynamo stadium. Promises must be kept. The statue had him sitting on a bench, and so I slipped the trophy in there beside him. He deserved it – it was his.

From that moment on, the memory of him in 1999 – his sad expression after our semi-final defeat by Bayern Munich – became a little bit sweeter. He smiled more. I smiled more. There has always been a part of him in me: the Colonel, too, had just become a European champion.

With Dynamo, he had managed to bring international glory to his country, winning two Cup Winners' Cups and a European Supercup. Dynamo have their trophy room, as well.

It was in that period that I was shown the results of a few fitness tests from my time in the youth teams there. They were part of a system created by Lobanovsky to allow the club to have a database of the physical condition of all its players at any given moment. From the kids right up to the first team. In this way, when someone got injured, a personalised recovery plan could be created for them.

That man was ahead of his time. 2002 brought the birth of Milan Lab, a scientific research facility based at Milanello that was the brainchild of Berlusconi and Galliani. I was more than happy to tell the story of Lobanovsky's database to Jean-Pierre Meersseman and Daniele Tognaccini, respectively the department head and project leader.

With those two at the wheel, I did a lot of training on my eyes. On a big screen, three colours would appear, and as quickly as possible, I was to touch the one they shouted out.

"Red."

"Yellow."

"Green."

"Blue."

"Violet."

"Orange."

"Indigo."

A full rainbow.

There was another version where different-coloured lights flashed on a wall. I refined my reaction times and my concentration. If you have perfect athlete's muscles but your brain reacts slower than your motor system, that's when the problems begin. Pirlo was brilliant at this kind of test – people said he had eyes in the back of his head.

I always had faith in Milan Lab. Often people don't understand that, with the general level of elite sport being so high, if you're not 100% right and lose form, your on-field performance will really suffer.

I draw a parallel with Formula 1: if one of your tyres is flat, you lose precious hundredths of seconds on every lap. Come the end of the race, you're miles off the leader. Soundly beaten.

The same thing happens with footballers. We need to be constantly checked and well maintained. If we get injured, it's better that we stop, otherwise it becomes impossible to heal and, by consequence, achieve results. The alternative is having to settle for second best, something neither me nor Milan especially liked. I had the feeling that the same went for Juventus.

The following season (2003/4) began exactly how the last one had finished, with us facing the *Bianconeri*. From the final of the Champions League, we had moved to the Italian Supercup, a one-off match on August 3. This one was played in the Giants Stadium, East Rutherford, New Jersey. It was boiling hot that afternoon. Dustin Hoffman and Donald Trump were both in the stands.

The scoreline was still stuck on 0-0 after 90 minutes. After extra-time, it was 1-1, with Pirlo having scored one of his dinked penalties a minute before Trezeguet equalised. On that occasion, the Silver Goal rule was in operation, which meant that if a team was leading at half-time in extra time, they won the game. Pirlo's goal arrived in the second minute of added time at the end of the first period, and at that point we felt like we had the game wrapped up. Instead, Trezeguet put everything back up for discussion seconds later.

Penalties again.

Thinking back to Manchester, there were more than a few similarities. But the outcome was different on this occasion: they converted all their penalties while Brocchi missed for us. A few guys on their side spoke about revenge for Old Trafford, but I couldn't agree. A Champions League is worth more than an Italian Supercup.

However, it's also true that defeat always hurts, a lot. And we suffered a lot of them that pre-season. Juventus beat us again, twice, in the TIM Trophy in Ancona and in the Berlusconi Trophy at San Siro. We had forgotten how to win.

There started to be a little agitation in the air, not least when we thought of the Stade Louis-II in Monte Carlo where on August 29 we would contest the European Supercup with Jose Mourinho's Porto, who had won the previous season's UEFA Cup.

Our whole state of mind was partially soothed, cured

and in the end transformed by the arrival of Kaka, who had officially signed that summer. Good news from another planet – there was life beyond earth after all.

Right from the very first training session, he left us open-mouthed. A 21-year-old Brazilian kid who did everything right. You watched him and couldn't believe your eyes. He never made a mistake. He had the inspiration, the class, the strength, the vision. For my type of game, it was an incredible gift to be able to count on a No.10 with his characteristics.

He would take the ball between the lines and carry it at high speed for 20 or 30 metres, right up to the edge of the area. Then he'd stop and look at me while the opposition defenders converged on him. At that point, he would pass me the ball, leaving me rather handily placed in a one-on-one with the goalkeeper.

He saw football like few others, he could read its rhythms and turn them in our favour. He turned up at Milanello already able to speak Italian. A great lad, very religious, well brought up. He was intelligent and alert, from a good family. Against Porto, it wasn't yet his turn. The task again fell to me. I scored after 10 minutes and the game finished 1-0.

I had started scoring again. A shot of belief for everyone, three days before the Serie A season kicked off. That night, after the official presentation, we partied with our families and friends and some VIPs. Laura Pausini, the Italian singer and a big Milan fan, dipped into her vast collection of hits to sing us some songs, and we sang along with her. We were out of tune but happy. In a certain sense, we were back at the summit of Europe.

PLEASED TO MEET YOU,
I'M ROMAN ABRAMOVICH

Ancona, Stadio del Conero. September 1, 2003. First Serie A match of season 2003/4. 90 minutes of Kaka, 90 minutes of Milan.

Two goals for me. Ancona 0 Milan 2.

A newly-promoted team against the reigning European champions. Kaka did not seem to perceive any difference between training and games. He always played the same way, effective and care-free.

His signing was a great piece of intuition from Leonardo, thanks to whom he had also been able to make a second-half appearance in a friendly against National Bucharest in Cesena 10 days previously. San Paolo gave their permission, even though the transfer had not yet officially gone through.

Kaka spent every day at Milanello. He integrated seamlessly and very quickly into a group that, after Manchester, increasingly resembled a block of granite.

We spent a lot of time with one another away from work as well.

In the meantime, Berlusconi kept throwing out a little teaser. "Andriy, you've not yet won the league here, right?" I had won five Ukrainian titles with Dynamo but, yes, in that sense my Italian record still had a big fat zero next to it.

Summer was coming to an end. The weather was pleasant, Milan exceptionally beautiful. It's an elegant city in all seasons. Kristen and I loved walking in the centre. Sometimes, we would stop to eat at the restaurant of the Four Seasons hotel, where I had signed my first pre-contract. One night we were leaving after dinner when a man came up to us speaking Russian.

"Good evening, Shevchenko."

"Good evening, sir."

I had no idea who he was.

"I am a football agent. Do you know Chelsea?"

"Of course, I do."

"Well then, follow me. There's someone who would like to speak to you for a moment."

Next to the bar, a man I had never met before was waiting for me. His face wasn't totally unfamiliar – perhaps I had seen it in a newspaper or magazine. He introduced himself. "Pleased to meet you, my name is Roman Abramovich. I bought Chelsea a few weeks ago."

He was kind, discreet, easy-going. Dare I say it, simple and straightforward. He didn't make a show of owning a huge empire, nor did he play on his status. We talked about everything, not just football. He congratulated me on winning the Champions League.

"Thanks for accepting this impromptu invite, Andriy."

"No, thank you, Roman."

We said goodnight, exchanging phone numbers. I began

keeping an eye on his club's activity in the transfer market and the team's results. Every now and then, we spoke on the phone or sent each other a text message. He was keeping an eye on Milan as well, from a distance.

We lost the Intercontinental Cup on penalties, against Boca Juniors in Yokohama. In the Champions League, we finished top of Group H, ahead of Celta Vigo, Club Brugges and Ajax. In the last 16, we knocked out Sparta Prague, before the quarter-finals brought something incredible.

After having beaten Deportivo La Coruna 4-1 in the first leg at San Siro, the second leg finished 4-0. To them. There was something strange about it. I don't know what happened, but they were running around like men possessed.

The best news came in the league, where we were going head-to-head with Fabio Capello's Roma for the title. We beat them twice, the first a 2-1 win at the Olimpico. I scored twice that day, and I consider the first one of the most difficult I managed in my career. Seedorf picked me out as I was running into the box, being tightly marked by Chivu. I controlled the ball on my chest, bringing it down and immediately striking it with my left foot, despite the fact I had the defender glued to me. On the slide, he tried to stop me.

The ball set off on a perfect parabola which caught Pelizzoli, the goalkeeper, off guard. January 6, 2004. Our epiphany. We played Roma again three games before the end of the season. Another party.

The party.

At 3pm on May 2, San Siro was completely full. Of emotion, and in every seating category. There was all sorts in the air, but above all a desire to bring home a trophy that had been missing for the last five years. We needed to be quick, and we were. One minute 19 seconds was all it took. Kaka, on the left, received a pass from Cafu. He set off on a run, leaving Lima and Dacourt in his wake. Then he crossed, picking me out in the middle of the box. I headed the ball.

Goal.

The goal that put us 1-0 up.

The goal that delivered the *scudetto*.

The goal that wrapped up Milan's 17th league flag.

A goal that was greeted by a roar I will never forget.

My 24th goal of the season, which earned me the top-scorer award for the second time. Parma's Alberto Gilardino was second on 23.

The goal was for Kristen, and not just her. She was four months pregnant. A son dearly wanted and hoped for. We were celebrating for three as I hugged her tight. As I hugged *them* tight. Not long before, I had asked her to marry me.

After we won the league, she asked: "What shall we do about the wedding?" I needed to switch off. I've always used holidays to recharge at the end of seasons filled with games and physical and mental toil. I was always exhausted going into the final mile.

"Kristen, I really don't fancy having to think about invitations and all the other things that take time and energy. The last two seasons have been intense."

"I agree."

We went to the United States for our period of downtime. Me, her and the bump that was beginning to show. We drove the west coast south to north from Los Angeles. We stopped off on the Monterey Peninsula and I played golf at Pebble Beach for a week, on courses that more than once have hosted the US Open.

We carried on to San Francisco, where we visited

vineyards and wineries. Then we flew to Washington, crossing America before visiting Kristen's family.

"Andriy, should we get married here, now?"

"OK, my love."

On July 14, 2004, I played golf with her father at the Congressional Country Club in Bethesda. It was a glorious day: the sun was shining and it was hot. We fought a close contest over the first 13 holes. I hate losing and he is the same.

I was in the middle of my career while he still carried with him the great character he had developed as a pitcher for the Minnesota Twins. Two athletes going head-to-head. Different disciplines, same work ethic. We got on really well, but whoever ended up winning was always that bit happier than the other one at the finish.

Kristen joined us with her mother on the 14th hole. And that's where we got married, all in the space of two minutes. The one dressed in white was me as I stood there in my golf attire. Kristen was wearing sporting gear too.

One kiss and on we went. Me and her dad, who had become my father-in-law mid-round, finished our game. We got changed and had lunch, at which point my wife's other relatives joined us. From that moment on, that's what I could call her: *my wife.*

I called Kyiv. "Dad, Mum, Kristen said yes."

It was a unique wedding that some might consider strange. But nothing was missing. We were happy, like in the fairytales that you read to children. But then the children grow up and the fairytales remain unchanged: fixed in time, space and place.

I got married playing golf, with Kristen in the place she loved and where she had grown up. We had no interest in putting on a lavish event; in fact, we used the rest of our time there to relax and talk. To plan our future, construct our family.

A life together. Love is substance and not appearance. It's heart. A look that only we would notice; an understanding that went beyond the number of guests. Love is saying yes and fervently wanting it until it happens. The rest is mere details. What counts is the journey you have been on together, and the road still in front of you both.

Love was me looking at Kristen. And it was Kristen stroking her belly, smiling at me.

Love was us three.

KRISTEN, I'VE WON
THE BALLON D'OR!

ROMAN ABRAMOVICH offered his congratulations on our marriage then told me something in confidence. "Andriy, I want to bring you to Chelsea and I'm going to speak to Milan about it. I've signed up Jose Mourinho as manager – he just won the Champions League with Porto. What do you think?"

He was doing things the right way. He wanted to put together a great team to win the Champions League. The previous season, they had been knocked out in the semi-finals by Monaco.

"Thank you, Roman, for the faith you're showing in me, but it's right and proper that the club decide. If the directors want me to stay, I stay. If they accept your offer, I'm coming to London."

I stayed. Berlusconi turned down a not insignificant sum and I signed a new contract with Milan. My last one.

Abramovich and I kept in touch. I even scored a goal against his team, in a 3-2 friendly win in Philadelphia's Lincoln Stadium on August 2, 2004. He didn't take offence.

After completing our summer training and as the start of the 2004/5 league season approached, I won the Italian Supercup at the third attempt. Having previously lost to Parma and Juventus, this time I tasted success against Lazio. In a one-off game at San Siro, we beat them 3-0 with me scoring a hat-trick. One more night of emotion to add to the collection. Nothing like the one I would experience two months later, though. That one was absolutely, spectacularly, positively overwhelming.

On October 29, my son Jordan was born.

We were due to head to Genoa for a Serie A match against Sampdoria the following day. Before getting on the team bus at Milanello, I called Kristen as I always did.

"How are you?"

"Not too bad, Andriy. I've just got back from the gym. My stomach is a little bit sore, I can feel small contractions, but I reckon they are just because of the exercises I was doing."

"Get some rest, then. Let's speak later on, when I arrive."

Forty minutes later, she was on the phone again.

"Andriy, it's happening."

"What is?"

"My waters have broken, they're taking me in."

I was in my usual spot, halfway down the bus. I got up and went down to Ancelotti in the front row.

"Carlo, we need to stop."

We were on the A7 motorway. All big bends and straights. At the first layby, the driver pulled over. We were always accompanied by two police vehicles, and so I got off and spoke with one of the officers escorting us.

"Can you help me?"

They were all really kind. One car stayed with the team on the journey to Liguria while the other began taking me back in the direction I had just come from. At the same time, Donato Albanese was making his way from Milan. I can't call him simply a friend, because he was almost a brother. One of the family. He picked me up at a service station and took me to the San Pio X hospital where Kristen was.

"Donato, get the foot down."

"Andriy, I'm already breaking all speed limits known to man."

We got there in time. The labour proved long and I continually paced the room. At one point I even broke out into a jog. I was more agitated than Kristen, who was taking it all in her stride. Jordan was born in the late evening and I was there to see it.

When I held him in my arms for the first time, I was thinking about all the people who had been in my mind in Manchester as I walked towards the penalty spot. But this time they were smiling. My wife was more beautiful than ever – an endless magic. A mum, with all her qualities and new focuses.

That night, I went home and slept for a few hours. In the morning, a club driver drove me to Genoa to meet up with the team. When I arrived at the hotel, I was greeted by a round of applause, we had our pre-match meeting and then we ate.

After lunch, I went up to my room and fell asleep. I didn't hear the alarm going off. Roberto Boerci, one of our masseurs, saved the day by banging ever more loudly on the door.

"Andriy, open up. They're all on the bus waiting for you."

"Just a second…"

I threw my clothes on, chucking stuff into my trolley case in big handfuls. When I got down to the bus, sure enough I was the only one missing.

"Sorry lads, it won't happen again."

It was my fault that we arrived at the Stadio di Marassi a few minutes late, but I didn't receive a fine. I knew I wouldn't be starting: the last 24 hours had been happy but frantic. Up front with Tomasson was Crespo, one of our summer signings. From Chelsea. Abramovich hadn't managed to buy me but he had given us him, on loan.

After 66 minutes, with the scoreline still tied at 0-0, Carlo put me on, along with Serginho.

"Andriy, are you feeling it?"

"Yes."

Ten minutes later, I scored the winning goal, following up a Serginho shot that was pushed out by the goalkeeper, Antonioli. It was the first goal I dedicated to Jordan.

I was experiencing a period of extraordinary beauty, my routine turned upside down by new rhythms and responsibilities. The great thing about becoming a parent is that you have to prioritise the little one's needs over your own. You start a new life, this time looking at things from a different point of view. You gain a higher perspective.

I loved it all. Kristen and I dreamed of having a big family, but as a son myself I began to worry. From Ukraine, where my dad and mum were, we started to hear a few strange creaks. Something was breaking. The politicians were fighting, but not in their usual way. The Orange Revolution was at the gates and biting, dangerous winds were blowing. Down the line from Kyiv, my parents tried to reassure me. "Stay calm, Andriy. Enjoy the little one and don't worry."

There I was, a son with my own son to look after.

A father with a father and mother to protect. There they were, grandparents and parents. A family trying to defend itself. All of us at each other's side and service.

I hoped for the best, that it would all be over soon. That it would turn out to be little shakes without an actual earthquake. Victor Janukovyc had been about to win the presidential election, but his contender, Victor Yushchenko, had managed to get the result overturned amid allegations of electoral fraud. It was Yushchenko who became president. New elections were held on December 26 and he took office the following month.

In the meantime, I had been declared the winner of another election: *France Football* had awarded me the Ballon d'Or. Officially, I received it in Paris on December 13, but I had actually been given the nod a little while before. One of the magazine's journalists had contacted me on the phone, saying: "Andriy, I'm letting you know that you are in the final three. The other two are Deco and Ronaldinho."

He then called me a second time. I had stored his number on my phone and it flashed up as I was dozing on the couch one night at home. I answered the call, but he didn't even give me time to say 'hello?'

"Congratulations, you've won."

I shouted my wife over.

"Kristen…Kristen…"

However, the voice on the phone was still speaking. One thing he said stood out.

"You can't tell anyone yet. I'll come to interview you, and you'll need to do a shoot for *France Football*. You'll then pick up the award in Paris."

As soon as I hung up, I shouted my wife over again.

"Kristen, I've won the Ballon d'Or!"

I told Jordan too, but as he wasn't yet two months old,

he was guaranteed to keep it a secret.

I told my dad. My mum. My sister. My friends, both in Milan and Kyiv. Galliani. Braida. Berlusconi. Ancelotti. Rezo. A few of my teammates. I whispered it to Lobanovsky, knowing he would hear me. "Don't tell anyone, though."

As I was under contract with Giorgio Armani, I tipped off Leo Dell'Orco, asking if he could sort me out a nice suit for the ceremony.

I looked out of the window and felt at peace. With myself and with the world. Since our family increased in size, we had been living in Villa Cademartori, in Blevio on Lake Como; on the other side of the water from Cernobbio, in front of Villa d'Este. We were in that little golden space, so precious and so silent.

Berlusconi loaned me one of his private jets, a Falcon, for the flight to Paris. On the return journey, Galliani was euphoric and we had a photo taken that to this day is close to both our hearts. The other components of the travelling band were Rezo, Leonardo, Milan's operations director Umberto Gandini, and Braida, who was staring at me. He smiled and nodded, as if remembering something nice. Indeed, he was looking at his mental scrapbook and a picture that featured us both.

I knew what was going on. He'd predicted this, that time in Kyiv.

"Andriy, you'll win the Ballon d'Or in this strip."

A UKRAINIAN HERO

OLEH BLOKHIN (1975) and Ihor Belanov (1986) were the only Ukrainian players to have won the Ballon d'Or before me. It was an honour and a privilege. A sort of joint embrace that took in them, history and my country.

Eighteen days after Paris, on the final day of 2004, my country returned this warm embrace. Leonid Kucma, the outgoing president, had awarded me the title of 'Ukrainian hero', the highest honour that the government can bestow upon a citizen.

During the ceremony, he said that our nation's international prestige depended on people like me. Victor Yushchenko, his nominated successor, had called to offer his congratulations straight after I won the Ballon d'Or. Once again, I took the trophy down to Lobanovsky's statue, just as I had with the Champions League silverware.

As a 'Ukrainian hero', I threw myself – heart and soul –

into 2005. There were targets to pursue, goals to reach. In the league, we were going head-to-head with Juventus for the title. Their manager was now Capello, who had taken over from Lippi.

On February 19, we played Cagliari in an evening kick-off at San Siro. The captain of our opposition was one Gianfranco Zola. My night lasted all of nine minutes; just enough time for one of their defenders, Simone Loria, to strike my left cheek with his head as I made contact with the ball. I had broken my nose on two previous occasions, suffered all sorts of injuries and undergone a variety of surgeries, but never in my life had I felt pain like this. It flooded through my system, as if it had entered my bloodstream. I felt it everywhere.

I fell over and got back up, feeling a bit groggy. I couldn't really understand what had just happened. I left the field, accompanied by Dr Massmiliano Sala, whose face went white the second he looked at me.

"How are you feeling, Andriy?"

"Did someone hit me? Who was it?"

"There was a collision…"

"Tell me who it was, Max. Tell me his shirt number so I can get back out there and see him."

I was mad.

"Andriy, are you sure?"

"Totally sure."

"Andriy…"

I took two steps towards the touchline and looked up towards the floodlights. I couldn't see a thing with my left eye. I turned to look at Sala with my good one.

"Tell me the truth, is it serious?"

"Yes."

Ancelotti subbed me, putting on Crespo. I went back to

the dressing room, where there was a large mirror. I stood in front of it and understood. I didn't recognise myself. The left side of my face was all collapsed in on itself, and the eye looked misshapen.

For every game at San Siro, there's an ambulance present for emergencies, and I climbed aboard to be taken to the Accident and Emergency department of the Niguarda hospital. I took my place in the queue – lots of people were waiting in front of me.

"Doctor, give me something, the pain's killing me."

"It's better not to. Let's wait until you've had your tests."

"It's too much."

Me, who had always managed to deal with pain. Who got injured without realising what I had done.

After a two-hour wait, I had a CT scan. They kept me in overnight for observation and Sala never left me on my own. He feared a sudden deterioration. The diagnosis report was never-ending; it was like a papyrus scroll.

"Comminuted fractures of the left zygomatic arch and the left maxillary sinus. Fracture of the left lateral orbital wall. Microfractures in the nasal bones."

In layman's terms, Loria had smashed me up. It hadn't been deliberate – that much was clear from the replays. The following day I was discharged and transferred to a private clinic, where I underwent surgery.

Zola called me. "It was a footballing incident. As Cagliari captain, I just wanted to say that we're all really sorry about what happened."

The operation took many hours, and I had several metal plates inserted. I reacted badly to the anaesthetic and was shaking when I woke up. I didn't feel well at all. They gave me a sedative and I tried to sleep. Kristen was by my side.

I could hear the traffic outside and it annoyed me.

The clinic was right in the middle of Milan. At 11pm, I jumped out of bed and grabbed Kristen by the hand.

"We're going home."

"What are you talking about? Have you gone mad?"

"I don't want to stay here."

"Andriy, stop it."

"Kristen, I need to go home and see Jordan."

She wasn't happy but she went along with it. Even she could not have stopped me. After the evening ward rounds, there was only one duty doctor left. I said the same thing to him.

"I want to leave."

"Absolutely not, Mr Shevchenko."

"You can't stop me. Tell me where I need to sign; I'll take full responsibility."

He called the surgeon who had operated on me and by now was back at home. There was nothing for it; I was absolutely determined. I jumped in the car and drove us to Blevio, with Kristen ever more worried. My sight was still obscured. I knew I was making a mistake, but my need to get away was over-riding all logic.

As soon as we got back home, I jumped into bed. My bed. With my wife and son. With silence all round. The following morning when I woke up, Kristen had a question. "Andriy, do you really think it was right for you to drive last night in that condition?"

"I drove?"

I couldn't remember a thing. The period of home rest did me good. Later, they told me that I had seriously risked losing my sight.

Juventus won the league, but the title would subsequently be taken from them following the so-called *Calciopoli* scandal. Milan finished second. Having been out of action since February 19, I returned on April 6 in the first leg of our Champions League quarter-final against Inter. Another European derby. Them again.

I had been training with the team for a couple of weeks. The Milan psychologist, Bruno Demichelis, had come to speak to me as well. He wanted to make sure I had recovered from a mental point of view as well. Healthy mind (in a more or less) healthy body.

During our training matches, my teammates were careful not to make contact with my face, while the doctor sought to reassure me.

"You don't need to be worried about anything. You're playing with five metal plates that they put in to protect you."

The final question, and the last word, went to Ancelotti.

"Andriy, how are you feeling?"

"I'm ready to play. Now it's up to you to decide."

He trusted me. I listened to my body and Carlo listened to me.

In the San Siro tunnel before we went out onto the pitch, Marco Materazzi attempted to intimidate me, saying some nasty things about my cheek. I knew him well: off the field, he was a completely different person. On it, that was just the way he was made, and I wasn't about to judge him.

What he didn't know was that I had come across a thousand Materazzis during my adolescence in Ukraine. He was a little angel compared to them. Precisely because I was thinking about all the things I went through as a kid, I wasn't afraid. A few things did happen between us on the pitch as well, though.

The game was tough. In the very last second of the first half, we went ahead through a Stam header. Fifteen minutes from the end, we doubled our lead. When we had a corner, Inter were marking zonally and we had done a lot of preparatory work to take advantage of those situations. Sure enough, we scored from a corner.

I scored the goal.

With my head.

Nearly with my cheek.

That cheek.

Every game was a new start. I cared about the ones against Inter even more deeply. I always took on the *Nerazzurri* giving it my absolute best, often scoring goals and always respecting them as an opponent. A huge respect. From my first day until my last, I considered Inter an excellent team. A noble adversary whom it was never easy to go up against.

On April 12, we played the return match. Well, most of it. After 74 minutes it was called off after a firework thrown from behind the goal struck Dida. We were winning 1-0, with me having scored. We were awarded a 3-0 win and I was happy that, as far as the statistics were concerned, my goal remained valid.

PSV Eindhoven were our opponents in the semi-final. We beat them 2-0 at San Siro, with me and Tomasson scoring. In Holland, things became a little bit more complicated. The scorebook shows exactly how:

Ninth minute, 1-0 to PSV, Park.

65th minute, 2-0 to PSV, Cocu.

91st minute, 2-1 to PSV, Ambrosini, with a header. Saint Massimo of Pesaro.

92nd minute, 3-1 to PSV, Cocu.

We were through to the final, on away goals. Our opponents would be Liverpool.

Have you ever heard about Istanbul?

ISTANBUL

SOMETHING strange had happened, out there on the pitch at Milanello. Judged from the future, it was a premonitory sign. We should have grasped it, but instead nobody noticed.

A few days before we left for Istanbul, I met a Serginho cross from the left, heading it right on the six-yard line. Abbiati saved and so I pounced on the rebound. Once more he kept it out, from a matter of centimetres. A remarkable double save. I immediately thought, "Next time I'm going to hit the ball harder; that way it will go in."

That little training match seemed just the same as the hundreds of others we had played over the years. Taken in isolation, pretty irrelevant.

We were a great Milan team, ready to face Liverpool at the Ataturk Stadium. We approached that game in an extremely calm frame of mind, well aware of our ability.

We weren't hiding away: we invited family and friends to Turkey. For me, with Ukraine so close at hand, that part was easy.

Everything was going well. The build-up was serene. Our hotel was beautiful, if not all that close to the ground. In a megatropolis like Istanbul, everything is far away from everything else. Even one dream from the next.

The atmosphere between us was ideal. Our morning walk-through on the day of the game was straight from the Champions League winner's handbook. We had just the right amount of tension to avoid being caught by surprise.

I had an intense personal memory of Istanbul. On November 17, 2004, we had played a World Cup qualifier there against Turkey. We won 3-0, with me scoring a hat-trick. Everyone inside the Fenerbahce stadium had given me a standing ovation.

By contrast, for everyone connected with Milan, May 25 would go down as the day the world went mad. And yet, it started out as intended. We were the only team in it. Kaka was flying. After a minute, we went ahead through Maldini. The wind was blowing in the right direction, with our standard bearer at the front.

I scored our second goal, but the assistant referee ruled it out – incorrectly – for a non-existent offside. It was a huge injustice, but we managed to get over it and look ahead. I set up Crespo to put us 2-0 in front for real. Then Crespo scored a lob to make our half-time lead 3-0. Our fans were signing, and so were the English ones: *You'll Never Walk Alone*.

It was a happy break, but there was no party, unlike what some have insinuated since. Poisonous lies. We kept telling each other that we couldn't let up – we were a group of model professionals.

In the second half, Liverpool set fire to our souls. Petrol and tears – those are also flammable. In the space of six minutes, the moon was turned off. A dark, dark night. Without any lights to guide us, we ran aground.

With 53 minutes and 24 seconds on the clock, Gerrard scored with a header. 3-1.

After 55 minutes and 23 seconds, Smicer scored from outside the box, the assistant referee waving a flag which his boss did not spot. Another clear injustice, this ghost offside. Shovelfuls of salt rubbed violently into our wounds.

Fear started to knock on the door. Incredulity, too.

After 60 minutes and 11 seconds, Xabi Alonso made it 3-3. The Spaniard's penalty was saved by Dida, but he knocked in the rebound. We pushed and pushed, trying everything we could. But there was nothing for it.

Extra time. Another half hour of trying. Thirty minutes to search for happiness.

Three minutes from the end, I saw Serginho crossing from the left. I headed the ball right on the six-yard line and Dudek saved. Inside my head I heard a voice shouting. My voice. *Next time I'll hit it harder.*

My mind flew back to that day at Milanello. A very recent memory, clear as day. A fraction of a second to memorise the treasure map. I looked at the Liverpool goalkeeper and imagined he was Abbiati. From less than a metre out, I struck the rebound cleanly… and he saved again. Crazy. We were going to penalties.

Dudek was moving about on his line. Right to left then left to right. He was jumping around, on our nerves. Dancing.

Serginho: puts it over the crossbar. 0-0
Hamann: goal. 0-1 Liverpool

Pirlo: saved. Still 0-1 Liverpool
Cisse: goal. 0-2 Liverpool
Tomasson: goal. 1-2
Riise: saved by Dida. Still 1-2
Kaka: goal. 2-2
Smicer: goal. 2-3 Liverpool

I took that old familiar path from the centre circle to the penalty box. Sleepwalking: a person walking on their own while life goes on all around them. Half the stadium screaming and the other half holding their breath. You're part of that other half. The ball in your hands, the outline of a second Ballon d'Or taking shape, or perhaps it's just a hallucination.

Dudek was jumping up and down, reaching out with his hands. He was still dancing, but a little less wildly than before. I ran my fingers through my hair, an instinctive gesture to caress my final thoughts. I looked at the referee, as I had in Manchester. My run-up started off fast then became slow. I went down the middle. The goalkeeper dived to his right, but his left hand stayed there in suspense and that's exactly what the ball struck. The space between Liverpool's everything and the nothing of Milan. The border. That strange place where a single centimetre can change your destiny.

The end of the story. The story of the final.

Saved.

Game over.

It was all so incredible. However, for the sake of intellectual honesty, I need to give Liverpool the praise they are due. Their fans – like ours, it must be said – never abandoned the team, not even for a second. When they went 3-0 down, they sang even more loudly. They roared their hearts out. One big push, then another, then another. They pulled the car out of the quagmire when it was about to break down.

About to. None of us – on the pitch or in the stands – thought that the motor was definitively goosed. Even as they suffered and sought to defend themselves, our opponents never stopped believing. They got back up after three blows worthy of a technical KO.

It would have been easier to close their eyes and lie down. But no. Their odds were 100 to 1 against. Maybe even 1000. But they clung to that chance and took it.

Only truly great players behave in such a manner. I remember Jamie Carragher who, England aside, wore only that Liverpool shirt his whole career. He was their Paolo Maldini. He was tired and in real difficulty – it was a miracle he was still on his feet. I managed to elude him late on in the game, he fell but still somehow managed to win the ball back off me through sheer force of will. He wasn't giving an inch. We lost, it's true. But it's also true that they won.

By contrast, the missed penalty was all on me rather than being about Dudek's save. I didn't open up my foot enough, and so the shot wasn't as angled as I would have liked. That said, the goalkeeper had been outrageously good in extra time. I've watched back his double-save from me 1000 times. I've watched the full game at least 100 times.

Some of my teammates threw away the recording of that horror show but I wanted to study it in detail. Nonetheless, the more I watched, the less I understood. The more I tried to explain, the more what had happened ate me up inside. An acid that was in danger of corroding me. I would wake up in the middle of the night, soaked in sweat. I would scream in my sleep, scaring Kristen.

For three long months, I was a hostage of Istanbul.

Of that open prison, with its guards walking around in red shirts with the trophy in their hands. My mind was becoming a madhouse. Either I stopped tormenting myself or I was going to need some kind of specialist attention. I resolved not to think about it anymore. *Andriy, give it up.*

It was hard, but I did it. Slowly but surely, my sleeping patterns went back to normal. Goodbye lead pillow. I stopped screaming. Liverpool had given everything. They had battled with their hearts. We simply could not have won that game.

SHEVCHENKO
V
ANCELOTTI

MAY 25, 2005: Milan v Liverpool at the Ataturk Stadium. The cursed final.

May 29, 2005: Udinese v Milan at the Stadio Friuli. The last game of the league season, with the top two already decided. Juventus first, us second.

May 31, 2005: Singers' XI v Golden Team for Children at San Siro. The so-called Game of the Heart.

I played in Istanbul. I sat out Udine, because of a calf problem. I played at San Siro – I was still in pain, but I couldn't miss that match. I was part of the organising committee alongside Richard Gere, who took me on a fun tour of Lake Como in his motorboat before I invited him for dinner at my house.

It was a charity match to support several projects, one of which was the construction of new schools in Tibet being overseen by the Dalai Lama's sister. Another was my own scheme to help orphans and prevent the phenomenon of child abandonment in Ukraine.

Ancelotti wasn't happy. Not about my participation in the Milan event, but the fact I had missed Udine. "Andriy, explain something to me. If you can manage to play against a bunch of singers, why not against Udinese?"

The truth was that, to play in the Game of the Heart, I would barely need to run. I could move about slowly, making sure things didn't get worse with my calf. A little walk in the park to show face. Carlo saw it differently.

"I think it's right that you take part in the San Siro match. It's a noble gesture on your part, a matter of honour. But I think you are just as duty-bound to play with us in Serie A. Therefore, I'm not happy with your behaviour. Know that I am disappointed."

Against Udinese, I would have been playing to win, and so pushing hard with the risk of worsening the injury. In the charity game, I would be playing for fun and to do some good, without asking much of my body. The calf issue was genuine.

Diego Maradona turned up at San Siro, and even in his civvies, he had a great influence on the occasion. For the first time, I was able to speak face-to-face with one of my idols. A straightforward, genuine soul, he cheered me right up.

"Andriy, enough about Istanbul. I know it was only a week ago, but you need to park your torment as soon as possible, even if it will take time. Football's like that, you can't do anything about it."

That little misunderstanding with the coach was still unresolved, a cloud hanging over me, when we set off for our holidays. As far as possible, I tried to relax, but it proved more difficult than anticipated. We were still in that period in which I was barely sleeping because of what had happened against Liverpool.

A week before the start of our pre-season camp ahead of the 2005/6 campaign, I took a call from the surgeon who had operated on me back in February after my collision with Loria.

"We need to take out the plates. The dentist needs to give you a little bone graft as well."

"No problem, professor. Nobody had told me. When will it happen?"

"Immediately."

"OK – when I get back, we'll do it."

"Get ready, Andriy – it's going to hurt. For four or five days afterwards, you won't be able to train."

As the team got back together at Milanello, I had the operation, which required local anaesthetic. I was in the operating theatre in the morning and that same afternoon one of the club drivers took me to the training ground, where my teammates had started work. We were scheduled to undertake a brief period of preparation there before heading to the United States for a tournament.

I met Ancelotti, we said hello and then he asked me a question.

"Andriy, why did you not have the operation before your holiday?"

"Carlo, I only found out about it right at the end of my break."

"How did it go at the hospital?"

"Good, thanks for asking. It's really sore, though. In fact, can I go home now?"

"No, you need to stay here in camp."

"What do you mean?"

"I mean that you have to stay here with us."

I went up to my room, slept for a couple of hours then tried again with the coach.

"Carlo, the doctor said that I can't train for four or five days. What's the point in me being here? It's better that I go home and have a proper rest."

This time he got angry.

"Andriy, I told you that you need to stay. End of story."

Another doctor had – quite inexplicably – told him that I could resume training straight away. A basic communication error.

And so, I called Galliani.

"Mr Galliani, I really don't understand. I'm really not feeling well, the pain is crazy and they're giving me a load of pills to try to make it disappear. I want to go home. Please."

"Ok, Andriy, go to Blevio and do what the doctor who did the operation told you."

"Thank you, Mr Galliani. As soon as I'm better, I'll get back to work. You know me."

And that's what I did. I was meant to take it easy for four or five days, but after two, I decided to return to Milanello and get back on the pitch. I wasn't able to train all that well, but I tried. I knew there was some tension. Maldini seemed cold towards me, Ancelotti too.

They all left for the United States, while I stayed in Italy to complete my recovery. When they got back, I was ready. The pain had almost disappeared, but the bonds inside the dressing room were not yet healed. At the end of one session, I called Maldini.

"Paolo, can we talk?"

"We need to, Andriy."

We sorted things out. The team had been given the same message that Ancelotti had received. They thought I was taking the piss.

"Is everything cleared up now, Paolo?"

"Andriy, go straight to Carlo. He's very unhappy."

That's what I did, straight after lunch.

"Carlo, have you got a minute."

"Yes."

We stepped out, close to the kitchens. I explained everything to him. As I did so, I gesticulated, moving my hands and swinging my arms. I must have seemed really agitated.

"Andriy, one of our doctors said that you could train straight away, do you know that?"

"Carlo, how could I have trained, with that terrible pain? I had incisions everywhere, my mouth sewn up, I could barely eat."

We embraced and made our peace. We carried on loving each other. What we didn't know was that some journalists were watching us from afar, filming us as they did so. They started saying that during our chat, I'd told Ancelotti I wanted to leave Milan. That wasn't true. I had only one thought in my head: to stay right where I was and try to win the Champions League.

Berlusconi invited me to Arcore. "I'd like to be Jordan's godfather." I was happy to oblige. On September 3, I played against Georgia in Tbilisi in a World Cup qualifier, and two days later came my son's christening. Kristen and I chose Villa d'Este as the location, and as Berlusconi was prime minister at that point, there were divers patrolling the lake and snipers stationed on the roof to guarantee his safety.

Among the invited guests were all my teammates and the club directors, as well as our families. At one point, Galliani took me aside and said: "Maldini is beginning to have a few fitness issues and Costacurta won't always be a starter.

Andriy, get ready to become Milan captain. Carlo and I have discussed it. When Paolo and Billy aren't there, the armband will be yours."

I was so happy I wanted to sing. Berlusconi beat me to the punch, grabbing the mic and singing a few songs. Ancelotti sang as well. He always did, when the chance arose.

And then came Galliani, with one of his party pieces: *Never friends* by Antonello Venditti.

> *Some loves never end*
> *they go on a long journey then return*

We were right at the start of my final season in a Milan shirt. But nobody knew; not even me.

DO YOU REALLY WANT
TO JOIN CHELSEA?

ONE of the performers at Jordan's christening was Eddy, a famous illusionist. Using his mind, he could move the hands of the clock back and forth. Berlusconi was very taken with him.

"As you know how to use it so much better than me, allow me to give you the one I'm wearing." He took the watch straight off his wrist and handed it to Eddy.

Time was running away from me as well, and fast. I'd kept speaking to Roman Abramovich: we didn't just talk about football. I knew that if I made it known I wanted to go to Chelsea, he would help me make it happen. But nothing like that had happened yet.

As Milan, we felt strong. Competitive in Europe as well as Italy. We still bore the mark of Istanbul but knew that every success would wash away a piece of it to the point where we were completely disinfected. We had bought

Alberto Gilardino from Parma, but at the halfway point in the league season, we weren't exactly well placed.

Juventus were on 52 points, Inter on 42, us and Fiorentina on 40 and Livorno (the big surprise package) on 35.

I started looking at my identity card. It said that on September 29 – which was also Berlusconi's birthday – I was going to turn 30. *Andriy, if you want to try a new professional experience, this is the right moment.*

That little voice was getting ever louder. I was torn. It wasn't a case of internal suffering, nor of a decision that had already been made. It was just a thought, especially at the beginning.

In the second half of the season, we managed to change gear and made the final table look that little bit more acceptable. Juventus 91 points, Milan 88, Inter 76, Fiorentina 74.

The *Calciopoli* scandal would rewrite the history of that season, with the title being assigned to Inter. It was a very strange year. There were certain games where, every time I set off towards the opposition goal, I would be flagged offside straightaway. Often the TV replays would show that I had been well onside, but there was no VAR in those days and so errors made on the field remained precisely that. There was nothing in the rules about correcting them on a pitch-side monitor.

If VAR had existed, it might have been us, and not Barcelona, playing Arsenal in the Champions League final on May 17, 2006. We had faced the Spaniards in the semi-finals. We lost 1-0 to a Giuly goal at San Siro, then at Camp Nou it finished 0-0. I had a perfectly good goal disallowed.

Merk, the same referee whom I'd not been able to stop

looking at before the decisive penalty in Manchester, gave a non-existent foul for my challenge on Puyol. He wasn't in the right position to make the call, and his assistant didn't help him. Puyol had slipped trying to stop me. That was April 26, 2006.

I would have dearly liked to help Milan reach the final, but I didn't succeed. It would have been a nice way to say goodbye, because deep inside, my mind was almost made up: I was going to leave at the end of the season to join Chelsea.

Over time, that simple thought had become something more. An idea. The curiosity and the desire to test myself in a different country, where I would be turning up as the top scorer in the previous season's Champions League. My European campaign had brought nine goals, which put me ahead of Ronaldinho (seven), Samuel Eto'o (six) and Trezeguet (also six).

I'd scored four of them in one match, away to Fenerbahce in the group stage. I'd previously scored a double for the national team in that same stadium. I could have ended up with more than four that night. At the end, after another standing ovation, I kept the ball. It's one of the few bits of memorabilia that I haven't given to my parents. I took it to my house in Kyiv and that's where it's always stayed.

Fenerbahce are a team from Istanbul. *That* Istanbul.

Missing out on the final gave me the push to make the change. I spoke to Abramovich. "Roman, I'm thinking about joining Chelsea. Are you guys still interested?"

He put me in touch with their chief executive, Peter Kenyon, who had a major doubt, or rather a total certainty.

"Andriy, we know that Milan don't want to sell you. If they let you go, we'll take you."

"What does the coach think?"

"We've just spoken to Jose Mourinho, and he's waiting for you with open arms."

I called Berlusconi, the man who had saved my father; the godfather of my son.

"I would like to go to England…"

"Andriy, think long and hard about this. We'll speak again soon. Come and see me after the game against Parma."

Ancelotti had invited all the team to a dinner.

"Lads, because my house in Felegara isn't far from the Stadio Tardini, you'll all be my guests after we play Parma."

That game, the second last match of the season, fell on May 7, 2006, a week before we hosted Roma at San Siro. I started and hurt my knee almost immediately, within the first few minutes, in a challenge with Fernando Couto.

I thought about Milan.

I thought about Chelsea.

I thought about the World Cup, the first one in history in which Ukraine would compete. Our debut was scheduled for June 14 against Spain in Leipzig.

I thought about myself.

A thousand doubts were swirling around my head. I touched my knee and shook my head. I then touched my knee again, and this time touched my head. Both were sore, for different reasons. An emotional short circuiting. I was no longer sure of playing at the World Cup; I was no longer sure of anything. I climbed in the car, and with that aching knee, I drove to Arcore. Berlusconi was waiting for me at his home.

"How are you, Andriy?"

"I don't know…"

"Listen, Andriy. I'll get straight to the point. Do you really want to go to Chelsea?"

"I've been thinking a lot about it. I think I want to

try a new experience."

"If that's what you want, I can't and don't want to stop you. I'll let you go for the sake of your own happiness. But know that everyone here wants you to stay. Milan is your home."

"Thank you."

"Get your knee tested then we'll see. But for now, get yourself to Felegara, because Carlo and the lads are waiting for you."

Once again, he had treated me like a son.

The journey between Parma and Arcore had been full of emotion; at times, the feelings were overwhelming. I was going to tell Berlusconi that I was off after seven seasons in the red and black. There was still a tiny element of doubt: when you're one step away from making such a drastic and radical change, you're never 100% convinced. We're not robots. The affection in which I held Milan and the whole environment was touching my heart yet again.

I had the exact same feelings travelling between Arcore and Felegara. Around the table, I would be sitting with Galliani, the team, the coach. All of them were well aware of the reason for my lateness. When I rang the buzzer, it was Ancelotti himself who answered.

"Milan house, good evening…" Here we go…

In the end, nobody asked me anything, because they all understood. It wasn't necessary to speak. We just had fun together.

I then went for another drive. Felegara to Milan, where a specialist was waiting to look at my knee.

"Andriy, you're about 60/40 in terms of needing an operation."

"Talk to me about recovery times, professor."

"If we operate, you'll be back on the pitch in two or three

months and you'll have to miss the World Cup. But even if you don't have the surgery, I can't guarantee you'll be fit in time."

"I'll take the risk: no operation. My whole career is wrapped up in that World Cup. I've earned it and I'm not going to lose it."

On the morning of August 12, in front of the doors of the prime minister's residence, Palazzo Chigi in Rome, Berlusconi had stopped to speak to some kids who were on a school trip.

He asked one of them, "How old are you?"

"Thirteen, sir."

"When I was your age, I was 15."

Another kid received a confession.

"Sir, will you say hi to Sheva for me?"

"But don't you know that Shevchenko wants to leave? That he wants to go to England?"

A very short conversation that was all round the football world in no time. The secret was well and truly out. Late afternoon that same day, I held a press conference at Milanello, all emotional. I confirmed that there was a possibility of me leaving Milan, adding that I was thinking of doing so for my family. I was struggling to talk. I was emotional. I was human.

For my last game, against Roma, I spent the first half up in the *curva* with the fans. The whole stadium started singing: "Sheva, stay with us." I was in tears. Everyone was.

Galliani then called me into his office.

"Sit down Andriy, and read this."

He placed a freshly-minted contract on the table. It was for five years, on the same salary that Chelsea had offered.

"Mr Galliani…"

"Sign it and stay here, in your home."

"Signor Galliani, I've already made my decision."

Silence. A long silence. His eyes were misting over and so were mine.

"Andriy, I'm going to ask you again: Are you sure?"

"I'm sure."

At that point, he called Abramovich.

"Roman, I'm here with Sheva: if you want, you can complete the signing, you have our permission. It's given reluctantly, however."

We embraced.

I went to Chelsea, but not for money. I gave Milan my whole heart and was honest with them from day one, even while making a few mistakes.

The decision was all mine; it wasn't a family one. I simply thought that it was the right moment in my career to make a change.

"Ah, Andriy, one last thing."

"Yes, Mr Galliani?"

"This is a 'see you later', not a 'goodbye'. Mark my words."

WORLD CUP 2006

WHENEVER I had to laugh and lighten my mood, I always thought back to a phone call that my friend Donato took one day. The memory was a good-mood pill that kicked in immediately.

I summoned it again in those hours when my transfer was being finalised.

"Good morning, is that Mr Albanese?"

"Yes, who's speaking?"

"I'm the mayor of Blevio, the place where Andriy Shevchenko lives."

"Ah…"

"Listen, is it you who built the miniature golf course at his villa?"

"Are we talking about Villa Cademartori, Mr Mayor?"

"Exactly that."

"Yes, it was me."

"Well then, can you do me a favour? Can you tell your friend Andriy that if he feels an urgent need to cross Lake Como straight from his house, he can use a boat? He doesn't need to make a floating bridge out of golf balls."

To practice my drive, I had bought 2000 balls. I hit them straight towards the water. They lasted a week.

"Mr Mayor, those balls are biodegradable."

"I know that Mr Albanese, but how can I explain that to the other Blevio residents? They don't believe it and insist that Shevchenko is polluting the whole lake."

Donato had to convince me not to buy another 2000. Regardless, the balls were indeed biodegradable. Thinking of that episode always lifts my spirits.

Generally speaking, golf is the thing that relaxes me. A few holes really help me destress, breathing that fresh air and walking in nature. I could do none of these things while I waited to find out whether I would be able to play in my first World Cup.

My knee was squeaking. Furthermore, my Chelsea medical was imminent. I was going to have to arrive at the club injured, not the ideal start to my new adventure.

On May 31, I flew to London with Milan's blessing. Things went well, I put pen to paper on my contract and Abramovich's club made the signing official. The first call I took was from Berlusconi.

"Andriy, are you happy?"

The second was from Galliani.

"Sheva, good luck."

Everything happened quickly. I briefly met Jose Mourinho, the Chelsea manager. He invited me into his office.

"Get fit and play for your national team. Let's just stay in contact. Depending on how far Ukraine go in the World

Cup, I'll let you know the date you need to report for training."

I continued my treatment, targeting our first group match on June 14 like an oasis in the desert. Water at last. I imagined the game against Spain, without knowing if I would play. It was a rope attached to a cloud.

I started training with my teammates only 10 days before that match. On June 8, I managed to play a little bit of a friendly against Luxembourg, my one and only action before the tournament. We won 3-0. I scored but was hobbling around. I wasn't 100%. I didn't even feel 50%.

I was Andriy Shevchenko in name only at that point, nothing more than a ghost of myself. To try to accelerate my recovery time as far as possible, I brought a small personal staff with me to Germany. It consisted of Piero Serpelloni, the physiotherapist whom Pirlo had recommended, and Endo Tomoroni, a Japanese masseur on loan from Milan. That was another lovely gesture from Berlusconi and Galliani, who let him come with me.

I was working exceptionally hard to return to a remotely acceptable level of fitness and form. Forty-eight hours before the Spain game, our coach asked to speak to me. He was Oleh Blokhin, one of three Ukrainians to have won the Ballon d'Or.

"Andriy, how do you feel?"

"I'm not 100% yet."

"If you don't play, you'll never reach the right level. I know you won't be able to play your best football, but you're the captain of this team, who are playing in a tournament like this for the first time. I believe you'll get better from game to game." He was telling me that I couldn't hold back. For Ukraine. For history. For him. For me. For everyone.

I was on the pitch from the first minute in truly atrocious

heat. We lost 4-0, with Xabi Alonso, Fernando Torres and David Villa (twice) all scoring. They destroyed us. We were a red carpet for them, the kings, to walk on. I couldn't get anything going. You could tell I wasn't right at all.

That result created a lot of tension in the group. Nobody was smiling and, from outside, the media snipers began to take aim. They fired all kinds of criticism at us. The defeat had been truly ugly, and we had turned ourselves into an easy target for friendly fire.

The situation could not go on like that – we were on the brink of imploding. As captain, I arranged a full team meeting, including players like Shovkovskiy and Rebrov with whom I had shared successful times at Dynamo Kyiv.

We promised to give everything we had for our shirt, whether we were injured or fully fit. From the youngest player to the real senators of that dressing room. A World Cup was exactly the wrong place and time to be scared, the wrong month to go into our shells. Every single member of the squad agreed with what was being said.

"We must stay united; we have the duty to act as a team."

We represented Ukraine, and Ukraine deserved respect and recognition. We were all her children. At the end of the meeting, I went to see Blokhin. "Don't worry, boss. It's all resolved."

On June 19, we played Saudi Arabia in Hamburg, winning 4-0 with an excellent performance. We had introduced ourselves to the world and extended a hand to the World Cup itself.

I scored a goal and contributed an assist. I felt better and understood that the coach had made the right call throwing me straight in there against Spain. If it was a gamble, it had paid off. In fact, it had been a safe bet to allow us to return to winning ways as soon as possible. The sun was shining again. Kristen – who was expecting our second child – came to join me, along with my family and that friend who had just got out of prison. On one of the days off that Blokhin gave us, we all went to Potsdam, the city where my father had served for 12 years with the army. His old house was still there, so we paid a visit. A return to his roots, a mouthful of oxygen, the story of his life before me. My sister had also been born in Germany, the same place where the Ukrainian team was being reborn.

A friend from Bergamo sent me a case of wine, and drinking a glass together became our way of cementing the bonds within the group. A toast to our World Cup.

The federation had chosen as our base a hotel just outside Leipzig and, after the meeting that had preceded our big win over the Saudis, we players started to meet much more often in the evening. A chat before bed to talk about tomorrow, to set out our next dream.

We split responsibilities between us. When the load is shared, it's easier to carry. That's the mathematics of the heart. That's exactly what we did against Tunisia, on June 23 in Berlin, in our last game in Group H. We won 1-0, with me scoring from the penalty spot. We qualified for the last 16, where we would face Switzerland in Cologne three days later. A truly endless game. Goalless after 90 minutes. Goalless after 120 minutes.

In the penalty shoot-out, our goalkeeper, Shovkovskiy, hypnotised everyone. I kicked things off with a mistake, but he finished the day a hero, saving from Marco Streller and Ricardo Cabanas, while Tranquillo Barnetta hit the bar. Switzerland were still stuck on zero, and we were off to the quarter-finals. Milevsky, Rebrov and Gusev were all successful from the spot to set up a match with Italy.

To reach the semi-finals, we would have to see off an

Azzurri side who, in their group, had beaten Ghana and Czech Republic and drawn with the United States before defeating Australia in the last 16. Their strength was the collective. They had won three World Cups before we achieved independence in 1991. The 1934 and 1938 triumphs had been overseen by the legendary Vittorio Pozzo, while in 1982, Enzo Bearzot was in charge. For me, it was almost a derby. I was the most Italian of Ukrainians.

We didn't win the game, but we left with our heads held high. Very high. Our opponents won 3-0, with a double from Luca Toni and Gianluca Zambrotta supplying the other, but we had several good opportunities to score. At one stage in the first half, I kicked the ground at the same time as the ball. I stayed on the pitch until the finish, but I'd hurt my knee again. That was June 30.

When we returned to Kyiv, people came out into the streets to thank us. Ukraine had just become one of the top eight teams in the world, part of the footballing G8.

Italy
France
Germany
Portugal
Brazil
Argentina
England
Us

So much pride, so many compliments. So many pats on the back, and then a few phone calls too. The first to call was Rezo. "I know you want to take me with you to Chelsea. Thank you for the offer, but I'm staying in Milan."

Piero Serpelloni called in tears. "I can't follow you

to London. My son has been diagnosed with a horrible illness." I was struggling to breathe: children should be untouchable, immune to any pain. He fought, they cured him and he got better.

Mourinho wanted a word. "Andriy, I'll expect you in camp in Los Angeles at the end of July."

Six thousand miles away. On the other side of the world. Far away from Milan. Which, for the first time, was far away from me.

NEW STRIP
NEW ADVENTURE

No holidays, that summer. Between coming back
from the World Cup and preparing for my move
to Chelsea, there was no time to rest. Not least because I
was trying to recover from the knee injury I had suffered
against Italy.

I was helped by Silvano Cotti, a physio I had worked
with in the past, and a newly-crowned World Champion.
As part of Marcello Lippi's staff, he was coming straight off
the *Azzurri*'s glorious cavalcade of triumph.

I was in excellent hands, but with my usual routine
turned on its head. For the first time, I would not get to
rest up for a month before starting pre-season fitness work
with my club. My body had always been used to that. There
really wasn't the necessary time to get myself into sixth gear
before the start of the new season. In a new strip. On a
new adventure.

Not even Silvano could work miracles in the space of a few weeks and so, when I reached Los Angeles, I felt tired and my knee still wasn't right. I felt really fatigued from the first day on the UCLA campus from which champions like Kareem Abdul-Jabbar (basketball) and Jimmy Connors (tennis) had emerged. Sporting gods.

I did my best and gave my all: that was just my way. Still, I knew my motor wasn't running as it ought to. Mourinho gathered all us players for his first address. "Lads, in my eyes you're all equal. I don't have favourites, that's not the way I work. I see no difference between big names and little names. It's simple: whoever convinces me the most in training will play. This is a group that can be really successful, and internal competition will do you good."

I understood straight away that he liked plain speaking. But the truth is I never managed to get into the right condition to make a serious impression, not even when we got back to London.

On August 13, 2006, I started the Community Shield – which pits the Premier League champions against the FA Cup winners. That meant Chelsea v Liverpool. I scored, but we lost a close game. The first possible trophy had slipped away. At the start of the season, that can happen.

Then the league began.

August 20, 2006. Chelsea 4-0 Manchester City. I didn't score.

August 23, 2006. Middlesbrough 2-1 Chelsea. I scored my first Premier League goal.

August 29, 2006. Blackburn Rovers 0-2 Chelsea. No goal for me.

September 9, 2006. Chelsea 2-1 Charlton Athletic. Still no goal.

Then the Champions League kicked off too.

September 12, 2006. Chelsea 2-0 Werder Bremen. Same story. Back to the league.

September 17, 2006. Chelsea 1-0 Liverpool. Another zero in my personal logbook.

September 23, 2006. Fulham 0-2 Chelsea. Nothing to report.

Mourinho called me into his office.

"Andriy, what's going on?"

"I know I'm behind. I still need to find my best form."

I threw myself back into the Champions League.

September 27, 2006. Levski Sofia 1-3 Chelsea. The long drought goes on.

League again.

September 30, 2006. Chelsea 1-1 Aston Villa. Once again: nothing.

By the end of September, the situation, at least for me, had become difficult to manage. I had had to deal with another muscular problem too. I didn't like not ever being 100%, because the fans and the club continued to support me in every way.

Mourinho gave me a warning.

"Andriy, every now and then, I'm going to leave you out."

"I know you need to make decisions for the good of the team."

On November 10, my second son, Kristian, was born in London. A huge, indescribable emotion; a carbon copy of what had happened when Jordan arrived. Positive days are always a new start, even when they repeat.

The newspapers criticised me heavily but only I knew the real problem: that accursed fatigue that had never lifted. I spoke with Mourinho again. "Jose, believe me. I don't need help. I just need to rediscover the freshness that I've lost."

It was nothing to do with mental freshness; purely

physical. Even if, sometimes, I silently asked myself certain questions like, *would it be better to go back to Milan?*

This restlessness was fleeting, because the choice to go to Chelsea had been all mine, and I have never been one to give up in the face of adversity. I gritted my teeth, worked hard, and trusted my muscles to Silvano. I never took a backwards step, either with my legs or my head.

Things improved in the new year. I could feel my strength returning and I started to see the light again. In February, we won the League Cup, beating Arsenal in the final. I was performing well and Mourinho seemed happier. "Andriy, you're back."

I started scoring again in the Premier League, FA Cup and Champions League, where my goal in the second leg of the quarter-final against Valencia was crucial. However, it seemed like it wasn't meant to be my season. Despite the more encouraging signs of the last little period, it had been cursed from the start.

On April 10, 2007, we won in Valencia, and on the 15th, we defeated Blackburn Rovers in the semi-final of the FA Cup. At the end of the game, another alarm bell was ringing in my body. I felt a pain in my stomach. I didn't know it yet, but there were dark days ahead.

In general, lists of dates are boring, but in this case, they show my ordeal. In training, I began to feel bad every time I ran.

On April 18, I didn't play against West Ham in the league.

We were getting closer and closer to the first leg of our Champions League semi-final, against Liverpool on April 25: an English derby placed right at the heart of Europe. God save the Queen and, if he has any time left over, perhaps he could take a look at me as well.

I was in pieces when that game arrived. Mourinho started me, while in the Liverpool goal was Reina. Dudek was on the bench: he wasn't dancing anymore. We managed to grab a win, 1-0 thanks to Joe Cole. After the game, the pain was even worse and I was examined by the club doctor. "Andriy, I reckon this is an inguinal hernia."

The second leg of the semi-final was scheduled for May 1 at Anfield. Before that, we were to play Bolton in the league on April 28. I was on the pitch but could barely stand up. I lasted 45 minutes of suffering, of withheld tears. Every time I ran, I wanted everything over, and indeed at half-time, Mourinho took me off.

The following day, another visit, another pilgrimage to his office.

"Jose, I can't do this."

"Listen, Andriy. Tomorrow we've got the last training session before we leave for Liverpool. Give it a go then we'll decide, together."

Ten minutes was enough. I raised my hand, signalling to the manager. Stop. A cold shower. Heavy thoughts. The latest trip to the boss's office, which by now I knew off by heart. It was an annex of my own home.

"Andriy, how do you feel?"

"I'm sorry, Jose. I can't run. Sometimes I can't even walk."

I wasn't picked. Indeed, my first English season finished there, with 14 goals in 51 appearances and many physical obstacles along the way.

Liverpool went through on penalties and the following night, Milan thrashed Manchester United 3-0 at San Siro in the so-called 'Perfect Match'. They were through to the final in Athens. Once again, it was Milan v Liverpool for European glory.

I couldn't be happy, however: Chelsea were out and I was

struggling with a physical problem that was truly annoying and difficult to resolve. It just wouldn't give me any peace.

It also stopped me playing in the FA Cup final against Manchester United. My teammates managed to claim a win that was all the more cherished due to the fact that the Red Devils had just won the league by six points from us. Another cup for Chelsea; our second after the success in the League Cup.

It was the Chelsea of Frank Lampard, John Terry, Didier Drogba. It still wasn't my Chelsea.

The newspapers gave me a lot of stick for missing the second leg against Liverpool; they reckoned I had pulled out at the crucial stage. It wasn't true; indeed, that inguinal hernia required an operation in Germany.

Germany 2006: I had been in paradise.

Germany 2007: I hoped to pull myself out of hell.

I owed it to our magnificent fans. I owed it to the club.

A SHADOW OF THE PLAYER

UNFORTUNATELY, during the operation, something didn't go to plan. I didn't get back to what I was before. My left adductor muscles weren't growing anymore and so my problems in this area became chronic. I lost strength. Something happened to the nerve and I lost some of the feeling. When I kicked the ball, it didn't feel like it should. And yet, I was fully intent on getting back to the levels on which I had always operated.

During my first year at Chelsea, there was all sorts of speculation about my performance. I would like people to understand that my difficulties were due to physical issues. The fans were great with me, but sadly I never managed to show them my best. I hadn't been able to play my kind of football with any sort of continuity, and sadly the second year was beginning in a similar vein, with a big hole at its centre. After the operation in Germany, I spent the summer of 2007 trying to recover. Unlike the year before, I did manage a holiday this time, but I always had the feeling that I was behind. I was working as hard as possible and achieving minimal results. I was putting in 10 and getting one back out.

Nothing changed when the competitive matches began. "Andriy, it's difficult to play you in this condition," Mourinho said.

Perhaps at the time I was unhappy and angry with his decisions but, when I became a manager myself, I understood. He was making the right choices for the team. A player will always want to play, even with one leg hanging off.

The league began and my role was invisible attacker. A ghost who scared even me. I wasn't there when Manchester United beat us on penalties at Wembley in the Community Shield. I was nowhere to be seen right up until the international break in September, but Blokhin still called me up for Euro 2008 qualifiers away to Georgia and at home to Italy. "You're our captain, we need you."

In the first, on September 8 in Tbilisi, I played 90 minutes as we drew 1-1. Four days later in Kyiv, we lost 2-1 but I scored. I felt better, especially against the *Azzurri*. I played well and was getting up to speed. As soon as I got back to London, Mourinho wanted to talk to me.

"Andriy, I watched your match against Italy on the TV and liked what I saw from you. Here in training, you look a bit behind. What changed between Chelsea and Ukraine?"

"In Tbilisi, the coach helped me. I needed to stay on for the whole game, regardless of how I played and my physical condition. Those 90 minutes helped me to build a good performance against Italy."

"Well done, you played really well. How do you feel now, tired?"

"No, everything's OK."

"Excellent. In that case, I'm going to pick you as well."

And so it proved. On September 15, he played me from the first minute of a 0-0 draw with Blackburn Rovers in the Premier League, and then again three days later against Rosenborg in the Champions League. We drew that one 1-1, with me scoring. Two days later, Mourinho and Chelsea parted ways in a mutually agreed separation.

There were never any problems between me and Jose. Sometimes I was happy, other times not, but I always respected his decisions as a manager. There was never any break in the dialogue between us. That was there from the first day we spent together right until the last.

The next man in was Avram Grant, who up until that point had been the club's technical director. In the past, he had been a manager only in Israel, including with their national team. Between November and December, I got a lot of game time, but I plunged into the abyss once more on one of the most beloved days of the English sporting calendar. Boxing Day football, a party within a party. First you eat (at home) and then you cheer (in the stadium). You unwrap your presents then, 24 hours later, you run into the stands.

At that point, us Chelsea lads had become the gift. We were hosting Aston Villa at Stamford Bridge. I was starting, and after we went 2-0 down, I brought us back to 2-2 with a penalty at the end of the first half and a right-footed shot at the start of the second. We then went 3-2 up thanks to Alex (I claimed the assist), and the game finished 4-4. An enjoyable battle for everyone except me. Five minutes from the end I'd felt a sudden pain in my calf. I couldn't push anymore. I was in a rich vein of form – the worst possible moment to suffer an injury.

Again. Another one. Yet another one.

Silvano Conti came to London to look after me and immediately noticed something.

"Andriy, this isn't a calf injury."

Indeed, it was a herniated disc, a problem linked to the previous unsuccessful operation on the inguinal hernia. I couldn't undergo another operation so soon after the last one, and so I spent three months trying to get better. I was desperate. I lost all my strength. I couldn't run more than 10 metres. My leg wasn't responding to instructions and after a few seconds my calf would tighten up.

I was undergoing treatment, receiving injections, trying to train. But it only got worse. I was afraid I was going to have to retire from football: a terrible thought that I would have run away from, if only I'd had the strength. The truth was I couldn't even outrun my shadow, and I was barely a shadow of the player I used to be. Everything felt so heavy.

I felt bad for the people and the club. I'd have given the world to return the affection they were showing me. Instead, I was broken.

Suddenly, after a few months, I began to get better. To get a grip on my body again, or at least some small part of it. Slowly but surely, Grant brought me back onto the bench, giving me a few minutes here and there at the end of games. Sometimes a quarter of an hour. Little pieces of apparent normality. I went to speak to him.

"What's the point in throwing me on for five minutes or thereabouts? Can I go and play with the reserve team? At least that way I can try to get back up to speed with the rhythm of a match."

"On you go."

Back then, the reserve team was coached by Brendan Rodgers. You could tell he was an exceptionally well-prepared coach who would go on to do great things. He helped me, allowing me to sample the special taste of the pitch again. He got me back on my feet and sorted out my mind as well, giving me back to Grant for the final part of the season.

On April 22, 2008, I was on the bench for the first leg of our Champions League semi-final against Liverpool.

Four days later, in the third-last league match of the season, I came on with nine minutes to go against Manchester United. We won 2-1, moving level on points with our opponents at the top of the table, even though they had a better goal difference.

On April 30, we knocked out Liverpool and qualified for the final in Moscow. Victory arrived in extra time, while I came on a minute from the end.

On May 5, we claimed three points away from home against Newcastle. Grant sent me on after 86 minutes.

On May 11, we rounded off the league season with a 1-1 draw with Bolton. I got the whole second half, scoring a goal. We finished second, behind United, who had beaten Wigan. We would go up against the Red Devils in the Champions League final on the 21st.

I did everything I could to stake a claim for a place in Moscow. I knew I wasn't in the right form to start the game, but mentally and physically I considered myself ready to come on and make a contribution.

A few days before the game, Grant gave me hope. "Andriy, you're looking good. Keep yourself ready."

However, I stayed on the bench for the whole game at the Luzhniki Stadium. Manchester United won on penalties. Cristiano Ronaldo missed for them while, for us, Terry slipped while taking what could have been the winning kick. The game ended up being decided by Van der

Sar's save from Anelka. I was disappointed not to get on, even more so to have lost another Champions League final on penalties. I went straight back into the dressing room, without even collecting my medal. There was no fallout; I was simply gutted that we hadn't managed to win, and therefore to give Roman Abramovich the success he had long been striving for.

As a Russian, winning in his capital city would have had a truly special, sweet taste. I was unhappy not to have helped him achieve that dream. When we got back to the hotel, he was there with us and we spoke at length.

I left for Kyiv, played for Ukraine then finally went on holiday. First to the Bahamas and then to Miami. I was in a bad way. New, excruciating pains were showing up in my stomach.

Two weeks before the start of our pre-season camp before the 2008/9 season, I began training on my own. Running on the beach. It was a total disaster. A friend advised me to be seen by an American specialist whom the NBA and NFL players all used.

After an MRI scan, he said the words that I had feared and hoped never to hear. "It's another inguinal hernia. The first operation was not a success and we need to do another one as soon as we can. I'll schedule it for tomorrow."

I immediately contacted Chelsea. "In 24 hours' time, I'm having surgery. I'll be late back to the camp. For a couple of weeks, I'll do my convalescence here in Florida."

When I got back to London, I chatted to the new manager, Luiz Felipe Scolari, Grant's replacement who in 2002 had won the World Cup with Brazil. "Andriy, just concentrate on getting better."

I took part in the team's pre-season tournament in China and Malaysia, but on the pitch, I was in slow motion.

My strength had vanished once more. Here we go again: frustration and embarrassment mixed together. The others were all fine and playing away, while I limped around and suffered.

That pre-season, we also played the Russian Railways Cup, returning to Moscow where we had lost the Champions League final.

On August 3, 2008, in the bronze final of the friendly tournament, we beat Milan 5-0, with Anelka scoring four goals and Lampard supplying the other. I came on for Anelka in the last 25 minutes. An image flashed through my head: Galliani singing at Jordan's christening.

Some loves never end
they go on a long journey then return

Galliani the singer.

Galliani the general manager of Milan.

Galliani who had long been madly in love with that club.

Galliani who had sent me a clear message.

"Andriy, if you need to play, we're here for you. We'll help you. We've already discussed it with Ancelotti."

Berlusconi told me the same thing.

I wasn't well; I needed to put myself back together as a footballer. That was the message I gave Abramovich.

"Roman, let me go back to Milan, please."

"If you feel that's better for you, I'll let you go."

Roman wants only the best for all his players, that much is clear. He gave me much more than I was able to give to him, held back by the continual injuries. That's a regret I carry with me.

On August 24, 2008, I became, once again, a Milan striker. On loan. Desperately searching for my soul.

A PROPHET IN MY OWN CITY

WHAT had I become? I had no intention of continuing to live like a ghost. My objective was to start playing football again. I considered a return to Milan to be my best, and wisest option. A familiar path to start moving forwards while looking behind me; a reassuring road towards home. The comforting embrace of old friends and a place that had healed me many times before.

Over my career, I had always watched back recordings of my games, to identify mistakes and work out how to correct them. At Chelsea, I had stopped doing it: I no longer recognised that striker in the blue shirt, dragging himself around the pitch, essentially hanging about, held back by pain. As time went by, the fear grew that I would never find the old Shevchenko again. I was living on memories at the exact moment I wanted to create a different present.

In Italy, I didn't get the No.7 shirt. That was Pato's and

it was right he kept it. I went for No.76, my year of birth, which was a way of wearing my 32 years on my skin. Visible yet silent, excluding the squeaks and creaks of my body.

Ancelotti was still in charge, while on the pitch I could admire close-up the talent of Ronaldinho, an absolute phenomenon. In training, I saw professionalism taken to a different level by David Beckham. Those who didn't know him spoke of his image, his wife Victoria, his obsession with looking good. The lucky ones who got to work with him every day spoke, instead, of an almost maniacal application, of a continual desire to raise the bar. Sweat and fatigue, running and exercises to raise the quality of a technique that was already ultra-refined.

Beckham really was an example. I appreciated the way he conducted himself and saw the role of a footballer. We shared a few dinners, and more than a few funny moments, like the time I invited him to my house to watch Inter play Manchester United in the last 16 of the Champions League. Also present were Beppe Favalli, Paolo Maldini, Alessandro Nesta and my friend Donato.

David had spent many years playing for the Red Devils and had remained a big fan. We, as Milan players and his teammates, aligned ourselves with him on the couch. The English won 2-0, and let's just say that some members of the group twice ran up to my living room windows, screaming 'goal!'

The house was on Via Ravizza, near to San Siro. One night, me, Beckham, Favalli and Nesta played a game of football in the small garden. Every now and then, the ball finished on my neighbour's lawn on the other side of the wall.

When this happened, we shouted 'ball' like you do when you're a kid, but nobody responded. Luckily, we had a few back-ups. We weren't exactly being quiet, and one or two shrieks may have slipped out. At a certain point, the doorbell rang. We looked each other in the eye, thinking 'right, maybe someone is angry about the noise we're making and has come to tell us'.

Sure enough, when we opened the door, my neighbour was standing there. With four balls in his arms. He looked like a juggler and didn't seem best pleased.

"Excuse me lads, are these yours?"

"Yes, Paolo…"

My neighbour was Paolo Maldini.

We burst out laughing. We had just found a new participant for our impromptu game.

"I'd like to play in defence, if possible…"

We were a good group and got on well. But my fitness issues persisted. I just couldn't catch a break. Sometimes I played, but mostly I didn't. I never moaned to Ancelotti if he decided to leave me on the bench; I knew that he was right.

I had a few muscular issues, especially with my back, which became so sore that I couldn't drive. I had bought a motorbike, a Harley Davidson. I managed the sum total of 30 miles on it before being forced to stop.

I smiled more when I pulled on the Ukraine shirt. In the qualifiers for World Cup 2010 in South Africa, I scored against England at Wembley and then in Zagreb against Croatia. Those were the nights that kept me going, that kept me mentally alive.

But it was still too little in comparison to what I'd hoped for, and nothing compared with the habits that I'd carved into the record books. The truth is that, physically, I was continuing to struggle.

Before I came back to Milan, Roma had tried to sign me.

I'd spoken to their transfer guru, Franco Baldini, and then the coach, Luciano Spalletti.

"Come here to us, Andriy. We want you."

"Boss, you are a person whom I respect a lot. Roma are a great club and playing beside a champion like Francesco Totti would fill me with joy. But I need to say no. In Serie A, my only shirt is red and black."

It was a pleasant chat, with beneficial effects. I felt important, appreciated, wanted. Even if in the end, the stats from season 2008/9 – the last of Maldini's extraordinary career – tell their own story. Twenty six appearances and just two goals, one in the UEFA Cup against Zurich and the other in the Coppa Italia against Lazio. Almost nothing, statistically non-significant. I hardly danced at all. I said goodbye to Ancelotti and went back to Chelsea.

I arrived back at Chelsea and said hello to Ancelotti, who in the meantime had been chosen by Abramovich as the club's new manager. I didn't spend much time in London. I'd worked with Carlo for years, and our professional relationship had become a friendship. However, I knew that it was right for him to make the choices that he believed were necessary and at that time I was certainly not at the top of his list.

We talked and he informed me that I wouldn't be included in the European squad. That meant I couldn't feature in the Champions League. On August 18, 2009, I replaced Deco with four minutes left in a league game against Sunderland. Then I took a phone call.

"Listen, Andriy, we're in the Champions League this year and we'd love to have you with us. Think about it."

It was Surkis, the Dynamo Kyiv president, who two years previously had appointed a new general manager at the club. Rezo Chokhonelidze. That Rezo. My Rezo.

I spoke with Carlo. "I'd like to go back where I'm wanted."

I then spoke with Abramovich, who understood the situation perfectly. There was nothing left for me in London and it was time to turn the page. I accepted Surkis' offer.

I jumped into a time machine, going back all the way to my origins. I was still disappointed not to have given Chelsea what they deserved and what they had signed me for. That regret stung.

However, in season 2009/10 I rediscovered Kyiv. My Dynamo. The feel of the city where I grew up, of the team that had launched me onto the big stage. Places, people, feelings that I knew like the back of my hand. Beautiful tastes, reflections of myself. Kristen and the boys stayed in England but visited me often. It was sudden inspiration. The start of a stimulating new, old adventure.

The manager was the Russian Valerij Gazzaev. As a player, he had won a bronze medal at the 1980 Olympics and as a coach, among other things he had won a UEFA Cup with CSKA Moscow.

I felt happy straight away even if physically I needed a little time to reach my best. I got a good vibe from the whole environment, and there was rediscovered pride in feeling useful and appreciated again. I was a proper, full-time footballer again, not a name surrounded by nothingness.

I was No.7 again. I had come full circle. My enthusiasm soon returned, and in the league, I scored straight away: a penalty in the very first match against Metalurg Donetsk. In the first month, my body – which by now was not accustomed to certain rhythms – struggled to keep up, but week after week, game by game, my legs grew stronger and my mind started to fly again. I was a prophet in my own city, as I had been many years before. A fairytale. There once was a man called Shevchenko – and now he was back again.

We played Rubin Kazan, Barcelona and Inter in our Champions League group. That music that goes straight to the heart – you listen to it and follow it blindly.

Against a *Nerazzurri* team coached by Mourinho, we drew 2-2 at San Siro. Back at home, on November 4, 2009, we went ahead after 21 minutes thanks to my goal. Four minutes from time, Milito equalised then right at the death Sneijder managed to turn the scoreline on its head.

Unwittingly, we were witnessing the gear change from a team that would go on to lift the trophy at the Bernabeu, beating Bayern Munich in the final. We finished bottom of our section, but with the knowledge that we had gone toe-to-toe with the future champions and maintained our honour. I knew I could make a difference again.

My back, which had given me so much torment in Milan, still played up now and again. I was advised to see Hans-Wilhelm Muller-Wohlfahrt, team doctor to Bayern Munich and the German national side. We spoke and he examined me. "Andriy, if you want to continue playing, I advise you to come here to Germany twice a month."

I was playing a lot of matches, and so the pressure on my back was increasing. My visits to Munich multiplied over the following period, to the point where I was going there five times a month.

Two hours 15 minutes there and two hours 15 minutes back every time. But it was worth it, because things were still going well on the field. I was a footballer again.

In the league, we finished second behind Shakhtar Donetsk, which gave us a spot in the Champions League qualifiers for season 2010/11. We ended up being knocked out by Ajax in the play-off round and so dropped into the Europa League.

That tournament is an ungovernable ocean, sometimes calm and often stormy. In the end, we did very well, even if that October, Gazzaev resigned after losing to the Moldovans of Sheriff Tiraspol.

His decision made me sad. We spoke, but he said there was no going back. The club hierarchy temporarily replaced him with Oleh Luzhny, before appointing Jurij Semin on a permanent basis on December 24, 2010.

We moved out of the cyclone in that self-same Europa League, finishing top of Group E one point clear of BATE Borisov. In the knock-out phase, we won 4-1 away to Besiktas (Istanbul again) and in the last 16 we eliminated a Manchester City team with players like Mario Balotelli and a coach of the standing of Roberto Mancini.

In the first leg of the quarter-final, against the Portuguese side Braga, I was struggling with a little injury and Semin started me on the bench. "You'll come on later."

Indeed, he sent me on in the second half as a replacement for Kravets. I was booked once and then a second time, for having struck the ball into the net after the referee, Kravets, blew to stop the play following an offside.

I never heard that whistle. The Lobanovsky Stadium was absolute bedlam that night – a riot of colour and sound. It was the first red card of my career. We drew 1-1 and I was suspended for the second leg, which finished 0-0. Braga went through to the semi-finals on the away goals rule. We were a good team and could easily have gone all the way.

In the league, we again ended up second behind Shakhtar, who also beat us in the Ukrainian Cup final. I finished the season with 16 goals in 32 games. A decent average again. We took revenge on Shakhtar on July 5, 2011, when we beat our eternal rivals 3-1 to lift the Ukrainian Supercup.

In season 2011/12, the third I spent back at Dynamo,

my back got worse again. On occasion, I ended up going to see Muller-Wohlfahrt twice a week. On September 29, 2011, I turned 35. That's old for a striker, but I still felt able to prepare in the best possible way and answer any call that came my way.

I was chasing a target: a place at the European Championships which would take place the following June right here in Ukraine, and also in Poland. Every now and then, my body creaked and moaned. Little foreshocks. Minor muscle strains. Passing injuries. And still my bloody back. Up until March, I struggled.

After that, I didn't.

After that, I could see the dream drawing ever closer. Me and Ukraine, me in Ukraine for the Euros in our back garden. I longed for it, I wanted it, I chased it. Right up until Blokhin announced the squad.

He listed five attackers:

Andriy Voronin (Dinamo Moscow)
Marko Devic (Metalist Kharkiv)
Artem Milevskiy (Dynamo Kyiv)
Yevhen Seleznyov (Shakhtar Donetsk)

The last name was mine.

Andriy Shevchenko (Dynamo Kyiv)

CAPTAIN OF A DREAM

I FELT happy again. A kid well on the way to turning 36. The captain of a dream. Almost a third-time father: Kristen was pregnant again. On October 1, Alexander would arrive as a little brother for Jordan and Kristian.

I was a footballer with an idea that was starting to take hold: if those Euros went well, I'd call it a day. Retire in a beautiful state, in front of my own people. I'd say goodbye with a wave from my own balcony.

Ukraine had been drawn in a group with Sweden, France and England, which meant Zlatan Ibrahimovic, Karim Benzema and Wayne Rooney, amongst others, as opponents.

Five days out from our first match, against Sweden in Kyiv on June 11, 2012, my back locked. Crippling pain passed through me and Blokhin was worried.

"Andriy, are you going to make it?"

"I don't know. I'm feeling better, but can we give it a moment?"

"Sure. You can let me know on the day. I'm in no doubt, for me you're a starter, but in this case, you need to decide for yourself. Nobody understands your body better than you do."

96 hours out, it was sore.

72 hours out, it was a bit less sore.

48 hours out, the pain had decreased again, but only by a fraction.

On the eve of the match, I was speaking to a friend on the phone, explaining my doubts.

"I need to be honest with myself. I'm not wholly convinced I can play in this condition. And I don't have time to nip to Munich to see Muller-Wohlfahrt."

"Andriy, I know someone. This bloke. A physio in Moscow."

"Is he good?"

"He's a phenomenon. I think he can help you. His name is Alexander."

"Call him, please."

By 8pm, he was in our hotel in Ukraine. I had never met him before, but this was a man who knew how to perform miracles. He treated my muscles for two hours; I went to bed with a slight irritation and woke up a new man. There was an incredible lightness in my spine and in my head. I don't know how, I don't know why, but I had managed to get rid of a double burden, physical and mental.

I was well. Properly well. I cruised through the final training run.

"I'm more than ready."

That's what I told Blokhin, almost shouting.

"Excellent, let's go Ukraine!"

I was so ready that we beat Sweden 2-1 and I scored a double. No longer weighed down, I was moving around like a dream. Ibrahimovic gave Sweden a temporary lead and then I broke loose. My first was a diving header. A magical flight. The second, also a header, came when that man Ibrahimovic was marking me.

My feet were on the ground, but the feeling was beyond belief. That full stadium, those proud people, those contagious shivers. I'll keep the memories inside forever. The players on the pitch were Ukraine. Those in the stands were Ukraine. Together, we won as Ukraine. An overwhelming emotion, an overflowing pride.

Many of the newspapers had depicted the match as a private duel between Shevchenko and Ibrahimovic, but they were wrong. Thanks to Blokhin, we saw it differently. You can't be a heavyweight fighting on your own, and that's why we played as a team. That remains one of the most beautiful, intense nights of my life. A battle cry that went straight into the history books of our national team. Whenever I thought of a grand finale, that's exactly the sort of picture that came to mind.

Tears of happiness. Tears and dignity. Tears on the last few metres of the journey.

For the second game, against France, we moved to Donetsk. Our opponents were stronger and won 2-0. I took a blow on the knee, and in our third game against England I only came on in the second half. We lost 1-0, even though Devic scored a perfectly good goal that wasn't given. The ball was clearly over the line, but at that point the technology didn't exist to do anything about it.

And so, we were out. We left the field with the whole crowd on their feet. I finished my career with a standing ovation, even if at that stage I hadn't yet made my final decision. My Dynamo contract had just expired, but before the Euros Surkis had offered to renew it. I was wanted in China. I received calls from clubs in the United States. I went for a clean-up operation on my knee, which had already been booked in. I left for my holiday and during the trip, I went back over all the different stages of my life.

I thought a lot about my relationship with the national team, a bond I will never lose. That jersey is special, unique. A constant shiver down the spine, made up of instinct and emotion, responsibility to myself and others.

I was very young when I started wearing it, at a time when it was far too big for me. I remember my first few steps defending our country: Ukraine Youths against Netherlands Youths, who had one player that stood out. His name was Clarence Seedorf. I thought that he would become extremely famous and that, one day, I'd like to train with him. When we were all grown up, we found ourselves as teammates at Milan.

In the space of a single season, because I was so young, I played for three different national teams. The right one for my age and another two for older lads. I played in a World Cup, in 2006, then in a European Championship in Ukraine and Poland six years later.

Defeats are part of this overwhelming story too. Against Croatia, in the play-offs for the 1998 World Cup in France Against Slovenia, in the play-offs for Euro 2000 in Belgium and the Netherlands. Against Germany, in the play-offs for the 2002 World Cup in South Korea and Japan. Against Greece, in the play-offs for the 2010 World Cup in South Africa.

We became a big team step by step. We've never been like Italy, France, England or Germany, where football is an important, established industry. Ukraine can't expect to qualify for every tournament, but we can give everything in our attempts to do so.

My career has consisted of highs and lows, but fear of failure has never been part of it. Failure would be refusing to try. And if you're going to try, picking the right moment is also crucial. In November 2012, a few months after I retired, I received an offer from Anatolij Konkov to coach the national team. (Now the president of the Ukrainian federation, he coached me in the national youth sides and gave me my senior team debut).

I said thanks but no. I didn't feel ready; it wouldn't have been right. I needed to prepare myself, study, understand. I couldn't have taken on such a sacred role without a staff, without a clear style of play, without a coherent plan.

I took my time and tried to do other things. I became a father for the fourth time: on April 6, 2014, Ryder was born.

In the end, the call of the football proved too strong. That football which chose me as a child. We are inextricably linked. Always have been, always will be.

And so, on February 16, 2016, I accepted an offer to join the staff of national team manager Mykhaylo Fomenko as his assistant. That July, I replaced him.

That same year I lost my father. I miss him terribly.

I have loved (and love) Ukraine.

I have loved (and love) Dynamo Kyiv.

I have loved (and love) Milan.

I have loved (and love) Chelsea.

After Euro 2012, I was walking on a beach in Antigua with my wife. Being by the sea relaxed me; I felt at peace. We stopped for a moment and I took her hand.

"Kristen, it's time for me to stop playing. If I carried on, what could I possibly achieve that I haven't already? I'm finishing now, in a perfect moment."

I closed my eyes. I kissed her.

We smiled.

My Sheva
Zvonimir Boban

WRITING about Sheva is easy: you just need to let the *slavenska dusa* (Slavic soul) come to the surface in all its raw and sweet expression.

I think of my teammate, my brother and the surname he carries. One that is huge for Ukraine. Taras Shevchenko was the poet among poets, the father of the fatherland that gifted us our *Rossoneri* superstar.

Between the poet and the player, there is a clear analogy; a link between their respective bodies of work. They were both thoroughly modern, and ahead of the times in which they lived and worked.

They both delivered materially, but both were also full of heart and absolute passion. Usually, it is hard to find a balance between these things, but Sheva's football and the essentiality of Taras brought glory to their sweet, golden land. In my home city of Zagreb, there is a little monument to Taras, but in my heart there is one of Andriy. I saw him for the first time in Zagreb, when Croatia played Ukraine in the play-offs for France 98. He came on for the last 20 minutes and caused us a couple of moments of real discomfort down the right, but we won 2-0. In the second leg, he tore us apart, scoring two goals in 20 minutes. It was just as well there was no VAR in those days: his second goal was ruled out unjustly. We went through and began a run that would take my little nation to third place in our first-ever World Cup.

That night stuck with me, because I'd seen someone who just wasn't normal. He was unpredictable, he had a fifth and sixth gear and always kept the ball close to his foot. That night, he showed us that strange little meander before he breaks into a sprint, the direct dribbling and the utter ease with which he could always find the back of the net.

Physically, he was a beast with the precision of a sniper. His game had all the easy grace of a true talent who grew up playing on a dirt track. Back in the dressing room, we were only talking about one man. "First there was Blokhin, and now they have another…" our coach said.

And then he came to us, to our beloved Milan. I was a bit like a big brother to him. At the start, especially in Italy, everyone needs someone who can give them a few survival tips in this strange new footballing world. Well-mannered, ultra-professional and with that kind face – he won all of us over immediately.

He had a few problems at the start, when he seemed to want to run more than he wanted to score, but he was soon doing the thing he knew better than anything else: being that killer in front of goal – being Sheva. Even when he faded out of a game for a few minutes, all it took was one little half-chance and there he was, scoring again. One little chink of light in the defence and there he was, heading the ball or shooting with his left or right. Sheva could score with any part of his body.

I didn't like it when he came back after Chelsea. I knew it was a bad idea but in the final analysis, it didn't cost him anything: everything he had done before was still majestic, unforgettable.

After his playing career, after that mental closure that we all reach through one thing or another, Andriy the boy became a man. With his American wife and four little boys, he's constructed a splendid family, becoming an excellent father and husband. And with his very own Ukraine, he became a proper manager.

What he did not need to become – what he's always been and always will be – is *slavenska dusa*. True and clean, full of endless golden fields.

And if I reflect upon it properly, I need to go back and correct the first few phrases of this tribute. In my life, I've had many teammates who were friends and few, very few, who were like brothers. When I think of him, I think of a dimension that goes behind either of these descriptions. Thinking of him, I think about life, about our time. I think of my Sheva.

Sheva, Van Basten, Kaka – first, first, first
Adriano Galliani

Aᴅʀɪᴀɴᴏ, what's that noise?" A group of young women were trying to enter my hotel room in the Ukrainian capital, Kyiv. Their knocking was getting more and more insistent, so I moved a wardrobe in front of the door to barricade myself in.

"Adriano…"

Back then, I was deeply in love with a RAI journalist, with whom I was on the phone. She was in Helsinki for work and I was in Kyiv, being hunted by these persistent girls. And yet I was working, too – on a secret mission for Milan.

On November 25, 1998, I attended a Champions League match between Dynamo Kyiv and Panathinaikos. I wanted to see Andriy Shevchenko – our big transfer target and future signing – up close for the first time.

He played terribly that night, but what really stood out

was the cold. I had never felt anything like it. It was cold enough to make you cry, and if you had tears they would have immediately turned to ice. At the end of the game, I had more than a few doubts. Sitting beside me in the stand was our sporting director, Ariedo Braida, and I asked him a pretty direct question: "Are you sure this guy is the man for us?"

"One hundred per cent sure."

"Would it not be a better idea to buy Rebrov, his strike partner?"

"No boss, trust me. It's all cool."

Very cool. Frozen, in fact. I went back to my hotel room to try to warm up, but the windows did not close properly. My floor of the hotel was run by a woman of a certain age, whom I asked for some covers and a heater. She had a different idea to warm me up and pointed towards a group of girls. I shook my head and explained that I was in love, but I don't think she understood.

Neither did the girls, who began to move towards me. I turned on my heels, went back to my room and locked myself in. They wouldn't give up, however. They were battering on the door, and because that didn't close properly either, I moved the wardrobe over as back-up.

"So then, Adriano, what's all this noise?"

"Nothing much; I'm moving room."

No covers, no heater, under attack and with the freezing cold coming in from all sides, it was the only night in my life I have slept with my coat on.

I would do this and more for Sheva because – even if I couldn't have known it then – he's not a footballer like all the rest. On the podium of the players I have signed, he's right there with Van Basten and Kaka. First, first and first. Three Ballons d'Or. My pride (and that of Ariedo) divided into three equal parts. When I think of Andriy, the first thing that comes to mind are his eyes, just before he struck the decisive penalty against Juventus at Old Trafford in the Champions League final of 2003. That look caused me great mental damage. A week after the win, we organised a celebratory dinner in Milan's Sforzesco Castle and I ended up on the same table as a renowned psychiatrist. I had to ask.

"Doctor, excuse me, may I trouble you for a quick consultation?"

"Certainly."

"Well, something strange is happening to me."

"Go on, Galliani."

"Since that night, I've been replaying that match over and over again in my head. Every time it gets to Sheva's penalty, I start sweating, I get palpitations and I stare at the television as if it's the last thing I will do in my life. I fidget, I wriggle, and I almost end up strangling myself with my yellow tie. Basically, I'm still scared he will miss it. I close my eyes even now so I don't have to watch. Tell me the truth: is this something serious?"

"No."

"What good fortune."

"Let me finish, Galliani."

"Ah yes, sorry doctor."

"I was saying that the situation is not serious; it's irrecoverable."

I'd only experienced that same fear once before: with Dino Zoff's save against Brazil in the 1982 World Cup when, right on the line, he kept out Oscar's header. Back then, I'd also felt sick watching it back as I prayed to the Lord above to not let the ball cross the line.

I also want to underline that I never sold Sheva. He

left for Chelsea of his own will, despite the best efforts of me and Silvio Berlusconi to prevent it. In 2006, after our penultimate league game away to Parma, our coach Carlo Ancelotti invited us all to his house in Felegara, not far from the Stadio Tardini where the match had been played. Andriy arrived a bit later on, for the end of the party, because previously he had met Berlusconi at Arcore.

The president wanted to dissuade him from leaving Milan, but was not successful. I can still remember the phone call.

"Adriano, I've failed. He says he wants to leave."

To think that a few summers previously we had managed to fend off Chelsea. Roman Abramovich, their owner, had invited me to his yacht which was docked in Portofino. The Pelorus, some 115m long. Up for discussion was the future of Andriy Shevchenko. Abramovich had sent a helicopter to pick me up at Milan's Linate airport.

Before we touched down on that floating city, I noticed a few rescue divers in the water.

"Oh them? Well, Galliani, those men are there in case the helicopter misses the landing pad," said Abramovich.

Soon enough, we got round to Shevchenko. He made me an incredible offer: 50 million Euros. I was struck dumb.

"Roman, please excuse me a moment, I need to make a call."

I moved towards the bow and called Berlusconi. When those sorts of numbers are bandied about, you are duty-bound.

"Mr President, they have offered us 50 million Euros for Sheva."

"It's not even up for debate."

"Thank you, Mr President."

"You're welcome."

I reported back to Abramovich, who had me flown back to Milan in the helicopter. Immediately after take-off, I gave the rescue divers a little nod of appreciation out of the window. You never know, do you?

I remember everything about Andriy. Every goal, every celebration. Every game, every little moment. I am particularly attached to a photo we had taken together on the private jet that took us back from Paris after he was awarded the Ballon d'Or in 2004.

Sheva was involved in many Milan successes and it was in part thanks to him that I developed what has become my own little vice over the years: sleeping, at least for one night, with the cups that we have just won.

Without my coat on, I hasten to add. And with the wardrobe in its rightful place.

How on Earth did you do it, Sheva?
Paolo Maldini

THE room with the hearth was our meeting place. The spot where all the little rivulets that made up Milanello came together. The place where, every now and then, Silvio Berlusconi would pop in to play the piano. The heart, and the heartbeat, of our training ground.

On November 5, 1997, a big group of players – including yours truly – gathered in that room. It was a night for sofa and TV; chats and anticipation. We wanted to watch Barcelona v Dynamo Kyiv in the Champions League. We wanted to take a look at a young striker whom, it was said, would be joining us sooner or later. We wanted to see Andriy Shevchenko.

Goal, goal, goal. Before half-time, he had already scored three. At Camp Nou. He was deconsecrating one of global football's great cathedrals in front of our very eyes. Somebody switched off the screen and put the remote control back in its place. There was nothing left to find out in the remaining 45 minutes. Goodnight lads, and sweet dreams.

Sheva would become one of us, and Sheva would need us. Indeed, when he first arrived at Milan, he was like a foreign body, at least in those initial weeks. He came from a different culture. For example, when he finished his lunch, he got up and wanted to head to his room. We had to explain to him that was not how it worked in an Italian club: we all got up together, only when the last player had finished eating.

He was used to a lot more independence and a lot less sharing. Now and again we played jokes on him: we would all stand up quite suddenly. Andriy would jump to his feet, eager to get away – always with 101 things to do. But, in fact, some people were still eating.

"Andriy, sit back down," we would say, and he would get angry. He didn't like being made fun of.

Out on the training pitch, he would complain because our sessions lasted an hour and 20 minutes. With Lobanovsky, his former coach at Dynamo Kyiv, he was used to doing three hours or more. We, on the other hand, would moan that in those 80 minutes, he didn't run at 100 miles an hour. Because he was accustomed to going at cruising speed over a longer period, he was much more about resistance than sprinting.

In Kyiv, it was survive or die, whereas in Milan it was a case of fire every shot you have straight away in pursuit of victory. He understood this and adapted very quickly, a clear sign of major intelligence. He absorbed our mentality and the rest is history. The rest is victory and glory.

Andriy hated losing, whether it was a Champions League final or a ping-pong game against the eight-year-old son of one of our teammates. When it came to potential success, he didn't see men or boys, only opponents in his way. He made no exceptions; offered no discounts.

He was a truly unique footballer, impossible to compare to any other player that the football gods have sent down – for his way of being, for the way he played, for his very instincts. When people ask me how Sheva scored his goals, I tell them to sit down and make themselves comfortable because the response will take some time.

Right foot, left foot, header, first-time, exploiting defensive errors. Using speed, cunning, his heel, his toe, a sudden change of direction. You can't confine him to any one category: Sheva is Sheva, and then there's everyone else.

One night I was at home watching TV. I stumbled across a programme showing all of Sheva's Milan goals. I said to myself, 'I'll watch a few then change channel – I know them all off by heart in any case'.

One. Two. Five. Ten. Twenty. Infinite.

I found myself constantly amazed. I picked up the phone and called him.

"How on earth did you do it, Sheva?"

"I just always wanted to win, Paolo."

Today, in the room with the hearth, there is a picture of him as well. With the Champions League trophy in his hand.

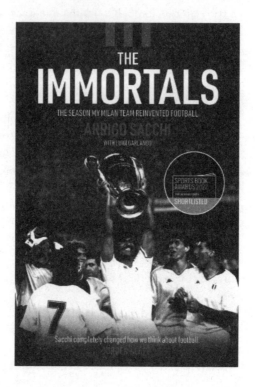

"Open the front cover of Arrigo Sacchi's memoir, *The Immortals*, and it will suck you in for a full day. The prose is dreamy and addictive"

Phil Hay, The Athletic

"The grandfather of modern football on his greatest season. There's not enough in the English language on/by Sacchi so this is gold dust"

Rob Draper, The Mail on Sunday

"Superb ... Curated from extracts of Sacchi's diary it gives a front-seat view of three seasons under the master tactician"

James Morgan, The Herald

 BackPage

"Pirlo's autobiography is like an erotic novel for football fans"
Four Four Two

"The autobiography of Andrea Pirlo displays a mischievous wit and an acute gift for observation"
Richard Williams, The Guardian

"Footballing autobiographies are not generally at the forefront of literary output, but this one is a superb read"
Jim White, The Telegraph